Taking Authority in Your Life

The Power of the Spoken Word

CHARLES ZAAGSMA

ISBN 978-1-63844-534-0 (paperback)
ISBN 978-1-63844-535-7 (digital)

Christian Faith Publishing, Inc.
832 Park Avenue
Meadville, PA 16335
www.christianfaithpublishing.com

Printed in the United States of America

Utter Defeat, No Hope, and Life at Its End—or Was It?

I was over at a friend's family farm. I was standing facing this typical-looking farm fence, gazing out into the horizon. It was an amazing scenery of rural country fields and hillsides with the sun starting to go down. It started to be a beautiful show of colors but not for me. I had just received a phone call, and the words I heard were devastating. I couldn't believe it. It was over. Everything was over.

It was another knockdown blow. I'm down again, and the hits just keep coming. This blow though seemed to be the one that would finish me—the last straw that broke the camel's back. I had taken many hard blows in my life, and I had always seemed to get up. I had always been a survivor—the last one standing after the carnage. From an early age, disappointment and death had reigned. My older brother and my younger sister gone before I even got out of high school. I knew there was a God, but I thought maybe he was an angry God. And he wasn't loving or caring.

My brother loved God and was so smart. He had gotten a full-ride scholarship to Gonzaga University for engineering. My brother died in his sleep at the dorm, right before Christmas, when I was a sophomore in high school. A month after my brother died, we found out my sister had a brain tumor. My sister loved God and believed he was going to heal her of her cancer, but she died anyway about a month before I graduated from high school. She had so much talent and was so amazing.

I shouldn't be the choice. They both seemed so much more than me and so much more to offer the world. Why was I the one left? I had been mad at God for so long now for, well, over twenty years. Even with him, it was just another bad and irreparable relationship in my life. I had done so many bad things. Maybe I deserve it. Maybe I deserve everything. Maybe I deserve his wrath. If there was a God, I definitely wasn't on his team. Maybe nothing matters. Maybe there is no rhyme or reason. Why me? Why am I the one who lived? Why was I left alive because I sure hadn't done any good with it?

If something is so bad, is it even worth anything? That was the story of my life. Was it even worth living? Why do bad things keep happening to me? I would always get back up, and I used laughter and humor to disguise and cover up my pain. But this time, the wind was completely knocked out of me, and it didn't seem possible to get back up or *ever recover* or ever even hope to feel somewhat normal again where I had always willed through everything even my will was gone.

The sky continued to be full of radiant color, orange, red, and blue, and the sun was starting to slip below the horizon. It was probably an extraordinary sunset, but for me it was anything but beautiful. All I could see was the sun setting on my life and nothing but curtains for me. Game over. Forty-two and my life was a fail. I had been officially damaged goods for some time now. I was broken beyond repair or so it seemed and looked. The man in the mirror disgusted me—overweight, old, so old-looking, and so ugly to me. I felt so old beyond my years, like I had one foot in the grave.

Everything I thought was important was gone. No one would ever want me or want to be with me. Every part of me seemed broken. My marriage, to whom I thought was the love of my life and the best thing I had ever known up to that point, was destroyed and ruined. Everyone and everything I love either dies or I end up losing. Why try? Every relationship I had along with three failed marriages were destroyed. I take the blame as I had self-worth issues and self-destructive behavior with a heaping side of deadly addictions that ruled me.

I had so much baggage pulling me down, and I was drowning without the energy or will to come back up. It was so much weight, and it would keep pulling me under. I could manage to just come back up to catch a breath but then back down. But this was it. I was going down. This was it—the end.

Emotionally, physically, and spiritually defeated and destroyed. All the king's horses and all the king's men couldn't put me back together again. I felt like I was better off dead anyways, and I was sure I was close to it. The world and my kids would be better off without me. What an embarrassment I was. Nothing good to show for my life, nothing but a path of destruction behind me as far as anyone could see.

My body was broken in so many ways, and this latest news added to the totality of it. So hollow and alone. Alone with no hope for change! It would cost too much to even have me in your life. Who would sign up for that? Who would even want to? I couldn't even work or even get a job like being a greeter at Walmart. Pain throughout my entire body. On the outside I was the life of the party, the "fun guy" (pronounced like the mushroom fungi), but on the inside I was so dark, hollow, and alone. I was an alcoholic and addicted to pain pills. The drinking and pain pills couldn't numb the pain anymore either, especially the emotional pain. How was I alive with what I would drink and the amount of pills I took? I wanted to die and felt I deserved to die. I wouldn't pull out a gun and use it on myself, but I was pulling the trigger on the bottle and pills—passive self-destruction.

Yes, it was suicide to keep doing what I was doing. This was the path I was on, and it was death for sure and soon at the rate I was going. I couldn't stop, if I could, I didn't know how. I kept trying. Every day I would say, "This is it. I have to stop, but I can't." I can't see how. How do I recover? It didn't look like anything would have helped. My body ravaged in so many ways. Damage in my spine that wasn't fixable according to doctors. Three surgeries between two shoulders. They had done all they could for me, but I still had multiple points of constant unrelenting pain including a knot in my back that felt like somebody stabbed me with a dagger. And it was still in there. Damaged vertebrae in my neck and nerve damage in my left elbow that controlled my pinky finger, ring finger, and middle finger of my left hand. I couldn't sit for more than fifteen minutes without my hand going numb and getting excruciating headaches. When I tried to elevate or raise that arm, I couldn't apply enough pressure to even wash my hair because of the pain. If I tried to hold that arm up too long or to try to steady something above my head, I would end up in bed for days, unable to move and in excruciating pain.

I wanted to give up and die, and I almost did. But that's not how this story ends.

Fast forward to the present day, a little over nine years later. I am clean and sober for eight years now. I am completely healed and restored to whole in every way. Since then, I have lost over 150 pounds and went from a size 4X to a regular size large and from a size 52 waist to a 32. With the very hand I couldn't control or use three of my fingers, I learned how to play guitar, and I played for the last five or six years on the praise and worship team at the church I attend. I cannot only control those fingers but can choose to move them independently and have the strength in them to hold down the right acoustic guitar strings on my guitar.

I also work on the maintenance team for our church, which also has a school and day care. The job I work at is very physically demanding, and I am enjoying a very active lifestyle. I am a whole package and overall more physically stronger and healthier both emotionally and physically than I probably have been my whole life.

My kids know me as a God-fearing, loving, good, and godly example of a man and dad. I'm married to my beautiful bride and wife, Pam, the true love of my life and the one that God had planned and designed for me. Many things that in my mind disqualified me actually make me perfect for her.

My oldest, Josh, who knew me at my worst, says I am the perfect example of God's grace and love. If he can change me, he can change anyone. The story I tell now is a different story. A story of love, joy, and peace. A story of life and life more abundant. How I am an overcomer and I now live in victory. My God is greater than any obstacle in my path. Death and defeat are no longer in my vocabulary, and they shouldn't be in yours either.

au·thor·i·ty
/əˈTHôrədē/
noun

1. the power or right to give orders, make decisions, and enforce obedience

We all have once we reach the age of accountability or adult-hood the authority in our life to "do what we want to do" and or control our "destiny" where we work, who we marry, etc. Most people will agree that they can make decisions for themselves, but they feel they have no control to give orders or enforce obedience to anything, so they eventually give up trying in different areas of their life and accept what they get or what they have. That's how it was in my life until I figured out I was sabotaging the outcomes in almost every situation with my words. I didn't know what authority was, but I was using mine negatively. Instead of giving up, I want to show you how to take back your control and authority like I did and start changing your life for the better.

> The most powerful and important part of changing your life is the story you tell about it and the words that come out of your mouth.

Choosing the Words to Tell Your Story

> My heart is inditing a good matter: I speak of the things which I have made touching the king: my tongue is the pen of a ready writer. (Psalms 45:1 KJV)

If you look at the root of the word authority, it comes from the English word author. The word author is usually referred to as a writer, originator, or creator of something especially a plan or idea.

The author gets to choose the words to tell their story, and they are the ones who create it. The author decides the focus and the outcome of the final product. Authors can create tales of adventure, filled with excitement, love, joy, and happy endings, or they can create sad or fearful tales of disappointment, disaster, and death. As the author of telling your story, you get to choose—not only do you get to choose your words but your words matter. You can choose words of destruction and death, or you can choose words of creation and life. If you choose better words, not only will the focus of your story get better but the direction and outcome will get better. No matter where you are in your story, if it's not finished, you can still change the ending—better words, better story, better life. Bad things or unexpected things may happen, but with the right focus on the desired outcomes you can and will prevail. You have control of more than your attitude. You can change your outcome and determine your destiny. Your story can matter to those who hear it. Your prayers can be answered. With your mouth, you can choose and speak life.

With your mouth you can release the creative forces of God.

You are a coauthor of your life with God

Yes, with your words, you can release the creative forces of God to change your situation and change the outcome of your life. With your words, you can tell the story of your life, and it can be the life that you want to live! Imagine that.

Yes, you can live the life you have always dreamed of.

The life God designed you to live…

Never Quit! Keep Playing! It's Not Over till It's Over!

Is your life story not what you thought it would be? Do you feel defeated? Are you knocked down and out? Well, you can get up every time you get knocked down, or you can stay down. It's not a nine-inning game or a twelve-round boxing match. There is no whistle or time limit to win. It's not three strikes, and you're out. You keep swinging till you hit the ball! If you're alive with breath in your lungs, you are still in it! Don't throw in the towel. It's your life. You keep playing till you win!

> For a righteous man falls seven times, and
> rises up again… (Proverbs 24:16 WEB)

No one has ever dreamed or desired a life of being conquered, defeated, broken, or just average—a life that is blah or no good at all. You were made for so much more. No little child says, "When I grow up, I want to be broken, mad, bad, and sad." If you can dream it, you can achieve it. If anyone had the right to stay down, it was me. My life and situation looked hopeless. I thought I deserved everything I got, but redemption freed me. And now I'm not just barely free but abundantly free. What God did for me, he can do for you, but it requires your part. Don't let your mind trick you. It's not easier to stay down. It is so hard to be defeated. Did I mention it's *hard* to be defeated? I'd say it a third time or a hundred times if it would make more emphasis, but I know I don't have to, if you are or have been anywhere near where I was.

We all have days, but when they turn into years and decades, hope gets lost. Don't let the world, the devil, your family, your friends, or anyone talk you out of your dreams or the goodness God has prepared for you. Especially you, don't talk yourself out of what is rightfully yours! The promised land is yours for the taking, and it requires your part for the possession of it. It's your life, so choose life and life to the fullest and overflowing. Remember that phrase "Choose life!"

Get Out of the Pot! Choose Life!

Have you ever announced something you were going to do, only to have others caution you and try to talk you out of it and say they "are just concerned for your well-being," and "they don't want you to get hurt." And then they list any number of things that could go wrong. Most of the time, people don't even say that it could go wrong, they say it will go wrong.

Think about crabs in a boiling pot, when it's well on its way to being over and when one is about to climb out, the others pull it back in and seal its fate with theirs. Misery loves company. Love people—but don't let them control your destiny or keep you at or below their level. You'll hear people say, "I tried that but it doesn't work." The world will tell you that you can't do something or all the reasons why and what you are trying to do will fail. They will put you down or pull you down to feel better about themselves or their situation. Their intentions may even be good, but only you "get to" decide your path and how you will blaze it.

Your life is a get to, not a have to! Most people are so checked out, that they are not only "not present" in their own life but are far removed from and "not present" in the lives of their kids' or their loved ones'. It may look like it's hopeless. Your back may be up against a wall, or maybe you've come up to what appears to be an immovable object. I have so many testimonies of things that God has done in my life that I thought were impossible! Maybe you got a bad doctor's report, maybe you have lost function in part of your body like I did, maybe you have lost a loved one or even lost the "love of your life," and maybe you're back in the search for a spouse, but it looks like you will never find that special someone to enjoy your life here on earth, your soulmate—the one God designed for you.

My wife and I didn't find each other until our earlier 40s. My wife waited her whole life for her "God choice." She had never married and had remained a virgin. Wow! What a gift from God. God will turn what the enemy meant for evil and turn it for good, but it requires your part of the equation to become reality. God's potential is given to you but not guaranteed. Yes, it requires you and your part. The waiting for the right harvest can be very hard but just like having the right numbers in the right sequence for a combination lock with the right mindset and the right words you can unlock your desires and receive blessing instead of cursing—yes life instead of death.

> But seek ye first the kingdom of God, and his righteousness; and all these things shall be added unto you. (Matthew 6:33 KJV)

While you are waiting for the added unto you, it doesn't make sense. If you seek God and his righteousness, everything else will fall into place. All the things you want and need are waiting for you if you would just seek what the creator designed you for and live and walk that out. The God of the universe can change your situation in an instant and part the sea in a way that you never dreamed. But if your words are stout against God, his hands will be tied, and your angels will be bound and unable to help you.

Decide now that you are going to claim the life God designed for you. Say out loud right now, "I claim the goodness God has for me right now! I receive everything God has prepared for me! It's mine and I receive it." It doesn't matter what your life looks like right now. God can take what the enemy meant for evil and turn it for good. Believe that! I am living proof! Decide now, and refuse to give up. Refuse to be average, and refuse the norm. Refuse to lose. Rise above the rest. It is not crowded on the extra mile because extraordinary requires extra.

Let me tell you the extra is worth it. Not being broken or a failure in the eyes of my kids and me being alive and present "in their life" is so worth it! Having the love of my life *in my life* is a value that you can't even attach a price. Yes, living your best life is priceless!

Most have given up. Having another round with the gang to blow off steam or drown your sorrows doesn't have to be the best it is going to get. Don't let anyone pull you back down into the pot or conform you to what is reasonable or what "they believe." "That's just the way it is" is a lie! It's easier for them to think "it's not possible" than that they just didn't try hard enough. Anything is possible to him who "believes." It's time to get out of your pot!

If someone asked you to describe your life story, what words would you use? Words of victory or words of defeat?

Victim or Victor: You Choose!

The difference between being a victim or victor is often just *the ending* and the right attitude and often just a few seconds on the clock. Not giving up when it matters…and it always matters. Champions are winners! A champion may suffer a defeat, but they will always get back up and rise above the situation. Even if a champion is taken out of the game, if they made Jesus the Lord of their life, it's just a promotion. You wouldn't feel sorry for someone who got a new job with a huge raise, awesome benefits and had to move to a new city. Heaven is a promotion!

Loss hurts, but there is always an upside if you look. As we delve deeper into creating a life like back in the garden or heaven here on earth with your words, you will see we are designed to be champions over every situation. A champion will focus on what they *can do*, not what they don't have or what was taken away from them.

Their words will declare victory, then they will seize it! Carpe diem! Tomorrow isn't promised, and yesterday is gone. Today is all you ever have. Seize today. It's yours, and you have it right now! You are already choosing the words to tell your story, but what words are you using? Do your words tell a story of a victim or victor? Do you sound like a chump or a champion? Woe is me or woo-hoo! Glass half empty or so thankful that the glass is half full. Did I mention I really like the woo-hoo?

You are what you are focusing on, and what you say about it really matters. You should speak like a victor! The word victor is Latin for conqueror! The perfect example of a conqueror is a king. Kings would rule the land and conquer other territories. In fact the word kingdom has to do with the king ruling or reigning over his domain or having dominion (same root word *dom*, as in dominant or dominate).

14

You Should Speak Like a King!

Thou shalt also decree a thing, and it shall
be established unto thee: And the light shall shine
upon thy ways. (Job 22:28 KJV)

A king is a perfect example of what authority looks like. Whatever a king says goes. He has power and authority, and what he says is *law*! Think about it, whatever you say is all that really matters to you. You have creative license over your life. It's your life, and *no one* can live it but *you*! You can be the victim or victor. You can't have both. You can't have sympathy and respect. You can't have someone feel pity or be full of sorrow for you because you're winning or being victorious! You get what you focus on. You will go in the direction you are pointing.

We all want to feel validated and not alone, but we are focusing on wrong things. Most people will connect and focus on all the negative and talk about what is wrong with everything in their life. They will constantly talk about negative things like how the traffic was so bad or why they never get a good night's sleep. Stop it! Try something different. Try the path less traveled. Try some umph in your life!

Yes triumph feels so great! Victory can be so sweet after a long battle. The harder the battle, the greater the victory! Let that sink in a minute... The harder the fight, the more satisfying the win is! You may have got beaten to a pulp and dragged through the gutter, but when you come out on top, it is so gratifying. Did I mention how good it feels to be on top? Two opposing adversaries could tell a similar story of how hard the fight was, but the only difference was how it ended. The victor has conquered, and now they are the king!

Remember what I said, "Life is not a nine-inning game, you *keep playing* until *you win!*"

> Where the word of a king is, there is power:
> and who may say unto him, What doest thou?
> (Ecclesiastes 8:4 KJV)

You have authority and dominion! Your words are filled with power and are supreme. So you should always speak positively about your situation.

> And the king of Israel said unto Jehoshaphat,
> There is yet one man, Micaiah the son of Imlah,
> by whom we may enquire of the Lord: but I hate
> him; for he doth not prophesy good concerning
> me, but evil. And Jehoshaphat said, Let not the
> king say so. (1 Kings 22:8 KJV)

Jehoshaphat was also a king, the king of Judah, and here he was telling the king of Israel that he shouldn't speak that way. Kings should want what they say and should say what they want. Most people already act like the lord of their own life where nobody can tell them what to do, but their words are wrong. A true king is a leader. Leaders just naturally lead. Nobody wants to hang out or follow someone negative. Down is not our natural state. A king should sound like a champion. A king will encourage and invoke bravery and stir up his people to fight for the things the kingdom needs life, liberty, and freedom from oppressing forces.

Proclaiming the Outcome
Before the Battle

One of the greatest examples of a champion and using your words correctly was King David, and the story of how he defeated Goliath in 1 Samuel chapter 17 of the Bible. This is also the story of two kings. Now David was just a boy, and this was years before he would become king. But he showed how the king is supposed to speak and act. Saul "who was the king" was in his tent "with his armor off" looking for someone else to fight his "giant battle." Saul and the rest of the army were frozen in their tracks and fearful of this dreadful giant Goliath. The entire army of Israel was hiding out believing the lies of the enemy that they couldn't win. Goliath, for forty days and nights, was continually taunting them.

The enemy knows when you are afraid and will get in your face and intimidate you, and that's when you choose, do I want to live in fear and defeat or fight to win no matter what. I would rather be taken out by a bully, than live under one. I would rather shoot for the moon and miss, than shoot for three feet and make it. It's always a life-or-death choice. Doing nothing is a choice and will seal your fate one way or the other. Bondage to doing nothing and living in fear of death is death—death to a life of freedom.

So back to David and when he showed up on the scene. David acted completely different from everyone else. Let's see how David responded to the trash talking that Goliath was spewing at the children of God. David comes in and "says" multiple times that he will fight the giant, and he tells everyone including the giant exactly what he is going to do to him and by what power. I encourage you to read the whole chapter, but let's look at how David "proclaimed the outcome" right "before" the battle.

Then said David to the Philistine:

> Thou comest to me with a sword, and with a spear, and with a shield: but I come to thee in the name of the Lord of hosts, the God of the armies of Israel, whom thou hast defied. This day will the Lord deliver thee into mine hand; and I will smite thee, and take thine head from thee; and I will give the carcases of the host of the Philistines this day unto the fowls of the air, and to the wild beasts of the earth; that all the earth may know that there is a God in Israel. (1 Samuel 17:45–46 KJV)

Woah! Not only did this young David proclaim defeat for the giant but for the whole army behind him as well. Now that's courage. David said that the Lord would deliver Goliath into his hands and that he was going to kill him and cut his head off and also that the army with Goliath would be food for the birds and wild animals. David was referred to as a man after God's own heart, and he, like God, called and proclaimed the end or outcome from the beginning.

> Declaring the end from the beginning, and from ancient times the things that are not yet done, saying, My counsel shall stand, and I will do all my pleasure. (Isaiah 46:10 KJV)

David saw his God as bigger than the giant problem he had in front of him. He "said" God was going to deliver him. This is important to remember to never run at your giant problem with your mouth closed and make sure you give God a way to move like only he can do. Look at what David said at the end of his statement about giving God glory. When we do the impossible and give God the credit, then the whole world will know there is a God! It's by God and his power that he has given us that we can do what we do, and it's also so he can be glorified. God is always looking for someone to show himself strong to.

> For the eyes of the Lord run to and fro throughout the whole earth, to shew himself strong in the behalf of them whose heart is perfect toward him… (2 Chronicles 16:9 KJV)

One thing I want to add here is to differentiate between David proclaiming the greatness of his God and Goliath "trash talking." Talking trash is not of God. You will hear the enemy spewing lies at you often, and you must respond and reject what is not for you. We will go into that in more detail later, but respond with something like, "No, devil"—or whoever is saying it—"my God is greater than this situation, and he will deliver me." Even if you don't know how, say, "I don't know how, but God will make a way!" It's best to say this out loud, but if you have to say it in your head, then do that.

Don't accept things that are not for you or not in line with what God has promised us. Most of the trash talk you hear is negative and just putting the other person down. "Talking the talk" about what you are going to do or accomplish or how good you are is one thing, and you should do that but just trying to intimidate by saying whatever to discourage your opponent is not right. Everyone has done it. You exaggerate a perceived weakness to mess with someone's head and get them off their game. Talking smack or speaking "bad" things over your opponent is the opposite of speaking life; it's corrupt communication. It's cursing their "fig tree"(Mark 11:14), unless it's the devil, and I encourage you to curse or tell whatever he is trying to bring into your life to die and come to nothing.

Why is speaking bad things over others or about others bad? This is especially bad concerning gossip, speaking behind someone's back, or even just repeating bad things that have happened to others. You can't handle a stove pipe without getting "soot" on you. Or let me say it like this, it's crude but really makes the point, you can't handle or touch a turd without getting it on you or coming away smelling bad. There are certain things you don't want to handle because it will rub off on you or get on you.

I once put this foam to seal a hole around a pipe that came into our house. The hole had been leaking water. I used this foam to seal it and to block air and water from coming in the basement, but I got the foam on my hands. Oh, it was so hard to get that stuff off my hands, did I mention it was hard to get off me? I scrubbed my hands for so long, and it took some of the skin off—certain things you don't want to "expose yourself to" or "get" on you. You want to keep toxic things off you. Trash talking like gossip is toxic and corrupt communication. It is not life and should be avoided. I used to be great at it, but I found an even better way than talking trash or smack to release victory in your favor!

Just like David, this is an example of proclaiming the outcome before and in the middle of the battle. One summer, a couple of years ago, when I was a counselor at kid's camp (first time being a counselor…wow! Me a kid's camp counselor…umm even a "church" kid's camp counselor…anything can happen), I experienced one of my greatest revelations about only speaking right words, and it turned out to be one of my greatest testimonies to prove that integrity in actions and words matter.

The competition between teams was pretty intense. There were mostly younger counselors that were very athletic and very competitive to say the least. Now I knew and had been studying faith and keeping my words right for some time now. One of the first things we did was create a song and chant for our team. I wanted to make sure the power of our words was in whatever we came up with. My cocaptain, Noah, was so awesome! We were in charge of the Green Team!

Noah is a very creative amazing young man, who is a missionary and was at the time home from going to Bible school in Belgium. Between the two of us and the kids, we came up with a few chants, but our main chant or song was "We're lean, We're green, We are the best team!" (Notice we stayed away from mean.) We would sing it and have fun with it every chance we would get. Anytime the kids would start to talk trash or speak negative talk about the other teams, I would pull them aside and say that we are here to have fun and glorify God. I had to do this because like Goliath, some of the other kids from the other teams started talking trash to us. So it's natural for our kids to respond in the same way.

It's human nature for someone to double up their fists if you come at them with your fists doubled up. Rising above and responding out of love requires a conscious effort. So I told them, "You can say all you want about how good you are or how good the team is, but don't put anyone down because that is a false way of lifting yourself up. We are here to have fun and glorify God." Let's just say there were lots of opportunities for our words and actions to be wrong. It looked like we were getting cremated. It was very hot, and I really needed to check my attitude a couple of times. If it would have been a real war, I would have been planning my exit strategy or calling on the radio for extraction. No joke, nobody likes losing or feeling defeated.

It's in the battle when determination and adherence to your values are when it matters. Now, there were so many ways to get points like finding "tickets" with points on them, winning games, learning the dance for the camp theme song, remembering all your teammates' names, etc., but again it "looked" like there was no way we were going to win the team competition. And out of the seven teams or whatever, we were probably in last by the "looks" of it. With the competition being so intense, and me wanting the kids to win, the opportunity to cheat arose several times. Mind you, Owen, my youngest son was with me and on my team. This was his first camp, and I wanted my son to have fun and a great memory.

I reject cheating just like I reject every other sin and all the other lies of the enemy. It's a lie to think that you can't win without compromising your values. One instance, just before bed, I heard my friend, Nick, who was a counselor, tell his kids that he saw a ticket with a bunch of points on it down by the beach. I heard the voice of the enemy say, "Well, you are usually the first one up walking around and praying, you could find that ticket and no one would know." I rejected that thought and said in my head, "No, I would know, and God would know. No thanks!" So over the days of the camp, we kept proclaiming our victory and "singing" how we were the best team and saying and singing our other chants about our team before lunch or whenever we lined up.

The other teams weren't really singing their team songs much, but we were having fun with it. And there was such a good spirit around it. I was having fun and really enjoyed talking with Noah when we got to talk about the awesome things that God was doing in our lives and some of the things I learned about releasing power through "our words." When the big reveal started getting close, of who the winning team was, there were whispers that we were winning. Could it be so? Surprise! Surprise! When they announced the Green Team as the winners, it was so awesome.

We were jumping up, down, etc. Here was the kicker though, not only had we won but we had just under a million points… "Say what?" The next closest team was 250,000 points away from us. And then I heard the voice of the Lord that said, "You see, the enemy tries to get you to compromise when it's no contest at all." The enemy will try to get you to look at what you have lost or don't have or that what you have is not enough and then try to get you to say and do what the world does. Lie, cheat, and steal because it's the only way "you're" going to get ahead.

> There is a way which seemeth right unto a
> man, but the end thereof are the ways of death.
> (Proverbs 14:12 KJV)

The dead ways and words of the world lead to places you don't want to go. I know I tried them all. They are enticing but not worth it. The King James Version of it is "it sucketh." They promise one thing but leave you with another and usually leave you feeling dirty, guilty, and full of shame.

The Big Lie!

Speaking of lies, a big lie told long enough is accepted as truth! We all know someone who has told a joke or story so long that they think it's true.

When it comes to lies, the biggest lies we tell, most often, are to ourselves! We will tell ourselves and others why something is preventing us from whatever we are trying to obtain, whether it's happiness, success, or whatever! The problem isn't just that we believe these lies but that they are actually hurting us and keeping us from the very things we want.

The biggest lie that is prevalent today is that words don't matter.

The world says that you can say whatever you want and there are no consequences. In fact, I remember this lie from my early childhood and goes like this, "Sticks and stones may break my bones, but words can never hurt me." What a crock! The truth is words can hurt, and they are so powerful. Some of my most painful moments came from words—messages of disappointment, disapproval, divorce, and death. The Bible has this to say about words:

> Death and life are in the power of the tongue: and they that love it shall eat the fruit thereof. (Proverbs 18:21 KJV)

So what God has chosen to reveal to us here in his word is that not only do words matter but the power of life and death are in your tongue and you will eat the fruit of your mouth. You *are eating* the fruit or in other words the output or consequence of your mouth.

Notice it doesn't say that the power is in God's hands or the devil's hands. You get to choose the power of life or death with your words, so choose wisely. Remember, choose *life*! You set your boundaries and limits. You will never rise above the level of your confession. If you say you can't do something, guess what, you can't do it. I remember a Henry Ford quote, "Whether you think you can, or you think you can't—you're right." Whatever you think about it, you will say about it. Whatever you say about it, you're right in your mind and you believe it; otherwise you'd be a nut.

The Power of Words

So there is power—the power of life and death—and it's in our words. Let's look at some of the most powerful creative words ever spoken. Now stay with me on this as I want to show you where "our" word power came from.

> And God said, Let there be light: and there was light. (Genesis 1:3 KJV)

> For he spoke, and it was done. He commanded, and it stood firm. (Psalms 33:9 WEB)

Wow! God spoke and things, wonderful things, yes, wonderful things, happened. God, our creator, created the universe, and he created us.

> God created man in his own image. In God's image he created him; male and female he created them. (Genesis 1:27 WEB)

When he spoke, things came into existence, and he called them good. And he named them. We are made in God's image—his likeness. When you see children, they resemble and act like their parents in many visible ways. Regardless of what you think, like your Heavenly Father, you are creating the world you live in. What are you naming and speaking into your life?

What are you calling into existence?

Are you calling your computer stupid? Or are you saying, "My car is a piece of crap and keeps breaking down," "My bad knee," "I am broken"?

We were made in God's image. We were made "to be" like him. So we are supposed to use our words for us and not against us. We are supposed to use our words to create and not destroy and words to bless not damn. Not bitter but sweet water only should flow from your well. Stop calling your ex and the mother of your child a psycho! Do you really want that craziness in your life or your child's life? People, children, animals, or pets will always live up to their names, so choose wisely. Remember, choose life! We should create a world we want to live in. Remember we have the power of life or death in our tongue. "With great power comes great responsibility"—yes, Spider-man quote there.

Diluted, Corrupted, and Unrestrained Power

If words matter, and they do, why do we not see the correlation so easily? Our words are corrupted and watered down so much that they are of no effect. Concrete with too much water will have no integrity and will crumble and be worthless. Kool-Aid or lemonade that is too diluted has no flavor and is not satisfying.

On the contrary, light concentrated or focused enough can be a laser that cuts through metal. Yes, your words can be like a laser or like a scalpel and cut precisely and divide precisely what you don't want from what you do want. Remember the lie words don't matter. The enemy tries to get to us when we are little to prevent us from reaching our potential.

Elephants, when they are little, can be restrained with a little rope. They try and try but can't get free and they give up trying, even though when they are older, they are much stronger and could not only break the rope but pull the stake out of the ground. Remember to keep trying and never quit! The enemy has blinded us from the power of our words, and now that we have complete authority to rule over our life and surroundings, we don't believe we have any power in our words, so we say things we don't mean. Our mouths are full of death. "That scares me to death"; "I laughed so hard I almost died"; "I'm dying to go"; "That desert is to die for"; "I'm afraid so"; "I'm dying over here"; and "You're killin' me, smalls!"

By deceiving us, we use our own words against us. We have the power of life and death in our words, but we throw our words around flippantly. Unrestrained power is so deadly so fast. The same electricity that cooks your food and runs your refrigerator, if it wasn't controlled or restrained, will kill you. If you touched the raw power and energy of the electricity that comes into your house, you would be dead before you knew what happened. The same fire that can heat your house, when out of the fireplace, can burn down and destroy your home and family in a matter of moments.

Just like fire and electricity, your words, unrestrained, are deadly. I have heard stories of people saying they would never live to see a certain age, and they died just short of that age. The devil doesn't have to kill or destroy you personally if you do it yourself. This kryptonite is given to us at an early age and trained to us by the "world system." Most of what we see in the world is tainted or twisted from the way God designed it or even down right perverted. The use of our words is a great example. Where integrity and "truth" should be in our words, it is completely opposite. Most of the vernacular or verbiage of our culture is completely opposite to the meaning, which it should be used. "Those wheels are sick"; "That's dope"; "That's wicked"; and "I'm killing it! You're killing it! We're all killing it!" We have death in our mouths to describe something we like or that excites us. This is wrong.

Woe to them that call evil good and good evil!

> Woe unto them that call evil good, and good evil; that put darkness for light, and light for darkness; that put bitter for sweet, and sweet for bitter! (Isaiah 5:20 KJV)

One version of that scripture says that those who do that call evil good and good evil are as good as dead.

You're killin' me, smalls! Yes, even jokes count. Get death out of your mouth! You may say, "Well that's no fun!" Remember, there are certain things you can't handle without getting their effects on you. With words, you have to choose life, not fun.

The devil is a legalist! Don't open the door for him to come in on you whenever he wants. That is what he does. Down the road, when there is no correlation to when it was said, that's when the devil will strike. I truly believe that God or the devil can't move in your life without words being spoken. If you want integrity in your word, you cannot be a jokester. Believe me I used to be really good at being a jokester and making "plays on words." Silly talk weakens your word.

One of the definitions of integrity is the state of being whole and undivided or internal consistency without corruption. Words like kind of, sort of, and you know what I mean are words and phrases that weaken your word as well. They are on the fence or wishy-washy! Even the word, trying, implies you are failing. As Yoda said, "There is no try, only do or do not!" You cannot say things that you don't mean. It confuses your spirit and your faith. The word of God says, "Let no corrupt communication proceed out of your mouth" (Ephesians 4:29).

It doesn't take much corruption to make something bad either. Cake batter with any amount of rat poison or something deadly ruins the whole party. Seriously would you want to eat cake, or anything for that matter, made that way with just anything thrown in? We are mixing death into our life, and most of us don't even see it. We are confusing ourselves and programming ourselves to fail. Have you ever got directions that were contradictory? Confusion leads to being lost and not getting to where you want to be. Are you where you want to be? If not, first take a look at your words and what you have said about it.

Have you ever had a shoddy wire for your computer or headphones or electrical appliance that would work intermittently or to the point it just wouldn't work at all? It's frustrating when you can't count on something to work. With no integrity or consistency in your words, there is no power in your words. They don't seem to be creating anything, but they are. You make plays on words, saying things you don't mean. Sarcasm isn't a language you should speak. It corrupts your speech and the outcome of your situations. You don't or may not even trust you or what you say. If you tell someone you are going to be somewhere at a certain time, are you there on time? Is your weight reported correctly on your driver's license? If you "say" you are going to do something, do you do it? Are you a person of your word? Remember God and his word are one. A man and his word should be one. Giving your word used to mean something when our country was founded on godly principles. It matters. Integrity matters. What does integrity look like?

> He that sweareth to his own hurt, and chan-
> geth not. (Psalms 15:4 KJV)

Integrity is when you keep your promises even when they cost you or it hurts. Showing up late basically says not only is your word no good but that you don't value my time or yours. One problem with not having integrity or "trusting" yourself is self-worth. If you don't value yourself or believe you are "worth" having nice things, you will believe you deserve bad things, or worse, you will self-destruct yourself and everything around you as a way of punishing yourself. Hurt people hurt people. That was totally me. If I don't value my life, I won't value anyone else's either.

If your prayers are failing or seemingly unanswered, it's because your words are not right or without power. When one of my kids is in trouble, I want my words to count and be effective when I pray. I want my word concentrated and powerful and precise, like a laser that cuts straight to the heart of the matter.

Saying wrong things will stack up against you. While you don't see any immediate or causal effects, like this for that, your words will add up against you. It is cumulative. It's not what you say once or few times, but what you say over and over. You may know in your heart or believe one thing, then speak against it when you are frustrated with your current situation. Consistency is where the results are. If you don't water your grass consistently not only will it not be green but it will die and wither. Vice versa whatever you water or feed will grow. Whatever you give attention to will be more prevalent. If you don't give positive attention and words to a relationship, it will die and cease to exist. You will always have what you say and confess. If you confess you love someone and show them by your actions that relationship will grow and flourish. If you are saying what you have, whether good or bad, you are going to continue to get more of the same.

I just recently caught myself watering a situation in the wrong way. You could hold a gun to my head, and I wouldn't confess that my memory was bad. I would when it came up "confess." "I always remember what I need to remember when I need to remember it or before I need to remember it," but I caught myself (this is why being aware of your words is important) when someone asked me something that wasn't really important, that I would almost automatically communicate to them that "I am not sure, I can't remember." *Do not* and *cannot* are two different things.

I started to realize I was saying it a lot. I was saying "I can't remember" a lot. In fact, I was "saying," I couldn't remember more than my memory was good. And just so you know, if you're wanting to improve your memory, here are few confessions that aren't exact quotes from the word of God but are based on them, "My memory is blessed" (Proverbs 10:7); "All things are brought to my remembrance" (John 14:26); and "I have the mind of Christ" (1 Corinthians 2:16) are good things to confess. By the way, when someone refers to Scripture, look it up. See what God says. Look at different translations, and see if it resonates with what was said and if it resonates with you. What you look at, think about, and speak matter. I will show you later how and why God's word in you matters.

More examples of words that bring wrong things or words that hinder, and I'm sure you have heard one or all of these… If I walk by cake, it makes my hips fatter. I don't have two nickels to rub together. The scale is not my friend. We can't afford that. I can't seem to get ahead. One step forward and two steps back. I'm afraid so. I'm afraid we won't be able to do that. I'm losing my mind! Even if it kills me, we're going to do it! I'm going crazy! I don't have a pot to piss in. They say your memory is the first to go, and there were a few other things. But I can't remember. Ha Ha! Doesn't matter how much sunscreen

I use, I always get burned. Bug spray doesn't work. Mosquitos love me and my sweet blood. Believe it or not, I have heard these recently by believers, who believe God, and know that their words matter. Getting our words right is something everyone, myself included, has to work on and continually check to see whether we are saying what we want to have.

True story, when I was younger, it seemed like every summer I got poison ivy, so I remember something to this effect being said, "If there is poison ivy and he walks on the opposite side of the street from it, he'll still get it!" I even remember saying it myself. And man, that wasn't fun going through that!

A very important part here to get is this—have you described what has happened (and it may have happened once or a couple of times), or have you just prophesied the future as well? Yes, you can negatively profess the outcome of the battles coming.

Examples: I always get sunburned when I go to the beach; it doesn't matter how much sunscreen I put on. Every time *blank* happens, *blank* happens. If it weren't for bad luck, I wouldn't have any luck at all. You just never know what God is going to do. Words like *every time, anytime, always*, and *never* are *blanket statements and aren't really true, but they* do *include your future!* Let's choose our words wisely and plant things we want in our life.

Your Life Is a Garden, and Your Words Are the Seeds

> While the earth remains, seed time and harvest, and cold and heat, and summer and winter, and day and night will not cease. (Genesis 8:22 WEB)

> Be not deceived; God is not mocked: for whatsoever a man soweth, that shall he also reap. (Galatians 6:7 KJV)

Words are seeds. You are planting them, and you will reap what you sow.

Are you planting weeds?

Words are containers, pregnant with unseen matter that can multiply and bring forth a harvest or manifestation of visual magnitude. We have all seen infectious laughter spread to everyone within hearing distance of a real funny joke. A word can be filled with so many things, like love or hate, excitement or disappointment, life or death, happiness or sadness. Words can build, or they can destroy. Words can inform, or they can confuse. The list goes on and on, but no matter what we are talking about, we get to choose what we say about it.

Think about it, you decide what comes out of your mouth. Is your mouth full of life or death? Is your mouth filled with positive things or negative things? You choose! What are you planting? What are you watering? In the natural world, the comparison is easy to see. If you want apples, you plant apple seeds. What are you harvesting? If you don't like the harvest you are getting, change the seed you are planting. Are you planting weeds?

When I was going through difficulties in my body, you would hear me always complaining about it and confessing it to anyone who would listen. So many people do it, and it's like we are just trying to fill the void of silence or connect with someone and that is the only way we know how. Unfortunately, most of us have learned that negative attention or being hurt or sick was the only way to get loving-type responses or attention from those we like, admire, or love. It's wrong though, and you won't hear me do it any longer. But before I knew better, I would complain about the pain in my ankles or pain wherever. I would be like, "My ankle always hurts when I do that" or "My back is killing me!" This next phrase used to be one of my favorites, "I'm sick and tired of being sick and tired."

I was watering the current situation and preparing for a future harvest as well. It was a habit for me to complain or get sympathy from others or even to get a laugh at my expense about something bad, and man, I could make people laugh. I felt good about bringing smiles and laughter to other people, but I was really injuring myself. You can make people laugh and be silly without negative behavior and words. I was telling about how bad things were and was creating more of the same. I kept planting the seed of pain and watering it, watering it too well, and it grew bountifully. I was creating what is called a self-fulfilling prophecy!

Self-Fulfilling Prophecy!

You can have what you say?

If God revealed himself to you and told you that everything you said was going to happen, would you change how you speak? I can hear someone after God told them that "Oh, that tickles me to death" or "Hell yeah!" If everything we said came true instantly, we all would be in trouble. Changing your words is a process and takes real work, but I don't want hell. And I don't want death, so I don't want to speak those words anymore because I don't want those things or their effects in my life.

What does the word of God have to say about self-fulfilling prophecy? In Mark 11:23 (KJV), Jesus said, "For verily I say unto you, That whosoever shall say unto this mountain, Be thou removed, and be thou cast into the sea; and shall not doubt in his heart, but shall believe that those things which he saith shall come to pass; he shall have whatsoever he saith."

Jesus has revealed a lot here, that not only can you have what you believe and say but that *you already have what you believe and say with your mouth.* Saying is so important. It says or refers to the saying three times and only says believe once. *You are going to have to focus three times as more on the saying as you do the believing.* Christians and most people don't have a problem believing something is possible or even what God can do, but what comes out of their mouth hinders, stops, and prevents them from seeing it for themselves.

"I pray, and God doesn't hear me"; "The devil is being relentless"; and "I can't seem to touch God with my problem." Are you praying (saying) the problem or the desired outcome? *You shall have whatsoever you saith! You should be praying or saying the answer and not the problem! The answer by the way is God's word. What God has said about it, is the answer.*

Also in Luke 17:6 (YLT98), Jesus says, "And the Lord said, 'If ye had faith as a grain of mustard, ye would have said to this sycamine, Be uprooted, and be planted in the sea, and it would have obeyed you."

Here Jesus is telling us how we should operate and pray and to be like him. Even if you had the smallest amount of faith (he referred to the smallest seed that his disciples knew about), he said that you would have said, and it would have obeyed you. When you have faith, you say or speak to things, and Jesus said they would obey you. We are to pray to the "root" of the problem. Everything we see physically has a root spiritually. Every symptom has a cause.

So, based on these two scriptures, God has said not only will things obey you by faith but you will have what you believe in your heart and say with your mouth.

Whatever you are speaking is creating either for good or for evil.

The two components of faith are what is in your heart and what comes out your mouth. This is what you have and what "you live."

The most basic definition of faith is what you believe and what you confess. This isn't just for Christians. The more I see and look at what people "say" and what "they have," the more it rings true. You'll hear people say, "It doesn't matter what line I pick at the store, I always pick the slow one."

And you'll hear someone else say, "Yep, that's just the way it is."

That's when I will say to myself, "No, it's not I reject that! I am always in the fast lane!"

That if thou shalt confess with thy mouth the Lord Jesus, and shalt believe in thine heart that God hath raised him from the dead, thou shalt be saved. For with the heart man believeth unto righteousness; and with the mouth confession is made unto salvation. (Romans 10:9–10 KJV)

Look at how that verse says "confession is made unto salvation." Confession always precedes salvation. So it is believing in our heart that we are made right with God, but it's the confession that results in the saving or salvation.

The Mouth and Heart Connection

You have to get your mouth hooked up to your heart and have good things in your heart. Like a sponge when it is squeezed, what is in your heart comes out of your mouth. I first heard this from my friend, Eric, and it goes like this. If I put an orange on the ground and put a board on it and step on it, what comes out? Orange juice because that's what is on the inside. Garbage in…guess what? Garbage out! What you look at, think about, and say matter! The words are the indicator of where you are at and the direction you are heading. They indicate what you are full of. I know you have heard your full of it, but what are you full of?

If your car gas gage didn't work, how would you know it was full? Easy you would put the nozzle from the gas pump at the gas station and put it into the "mouth of the car" and pump till the nozzle kicks off from being full or the gas starts overflowing or coming out. When you keep pumping something into something, it will fill up, and when it's full, it will start to overflow. What is in you is overflowing out of your mouth. What is coming out your mouth is an indicator of what is in you. Also, what you say today affects what you believe and say tomorrow. What you *have* today is what you sowed or planted or what you believed and said yesterday.

A good man out of the good treasure of his heart bringeth forth that which is good; and an evil man out of the evil treasure of his heart bringeth forth that which is evil: for of the abundance of the heart his mouth speaketh. (Luke 6:45 KJV)

Whatever is deposited in you is whatever you bring forth, both good and evil. It's an easy concept. What you put in is what will come out. If you like a certain topic or hobby, you probably read all you can about it, spend time researching and doing it, and talk about it all the time. The information or words probably just flow out of you easily without any effort. My son, Zachary, loves airsoft and guns, and if you're around him any length of time, you are going to hear about them. My son, Xander, loves guitars and video games, so when he talks to you that is what you'll hear. Whatever you are passionate about gets planted in abundance within you and will come out of you.

If you want good things or a good harvest to be brought forth in your life, you have to plant good things. You can't plant thistles and thorns and expected strawberries.

In the book of Mark, Jesus said how things are planted or sown in your heart:

> The sower soweth the word. And these are they by the way side, where the word is sown; but when they have heard, Satan cometh imme- diately, and taketh away the word that was sown in their hearts. (Mark 4:14–15 KJV)

Now here, Jesus is referring specifically to the Word of God or God's spoken word. But what this reveals is that words are spoken, and they are sown and sown into the heart. Note here also when you get that word from the Lord, Satan comes immediately to try and steal it from you before it has a chance to grow and be established in you. He always tries to make you think that what God has said is not true so you won't believe. Also faith comes by hearing and hearing (by the word of God; Romans 10:17). So if words and faith are sown by hearing, what are you listening to and planting in your heart? Fear and doubt come by hearing as well. You might hear, "You might as well give up," or "It's okay. No one expects you to do it." If you hear something, it's your choice to receive it. You are an accumulation of everything you have ever heard, observed, or experienced—what you have planted (said) and what others have planted or said into your life.

The word of God is incorruptible seed or the perfect thing to plant, and on the other end, you have what is opposite to what God says. The opposite of what God says is corruption and death and or separation from God and his benefits. You know sometimes we think "we are bad" that we have so much darkness in our life. Darkness and its effects are really just the absence of light. Your life is at the level of how much light or God you've allowed into your life. It could be a sunny day, but if you stay in your house with lights off and the curtains pulled, it's going to be dark.

The darkness cannot stay when you open up to the light though. In truth, the darkness cannot resist the light. If you flip on the light switch in a dark room, the darkness can't stay, assuming there is power connected to the light switch, and the bulb is functioning or not burnt out. Make sure you're connected to the source and not burnt out. When you plant the Word of God in your heart, you will start to see the manifestation of it in your life. The good will start to flow out of your mouth like when your gas tank is full on your car and the gas starts to overflow if you keep pumping or putting it in. If you keep putting good in, the good will come out eventually. You choose your fruit or the harvest of your "seed" based on the words you choose. You get to choose life or death with your tongue.

Choosing your words is so critical in every area of your life. If you say your child is never going to amount to anything or end up in jail and when it happens, you say, "I told you so!" You weren't predicting the future, you were creating it. You professed it and made it a prophecy. You proclaimed the outcome. You planted the seed, watered it, and cultivated the harvest of your words. You spoke things into existence.

You may have a situation that is or seems out of control, but do not confirm it or "come in agreement" with it by telling everyone about it. Your kid may not be listening to you, but don't say, "You're not listening!" "You never listen" is even worse. You should say something like, "Thank you for listening and obeying me." Whatever you do, don't and, I see this all the time, go telling all your friends about how your kids "never listen" to you or how they "are driving you crazy" or "my kids are out of control."

You are and will be bound by your words.

In Proverbs 6:2 it says, "You are snared or caught by your words."

> You are trapped by the words of your mouth.
> You are ensnared with the words of your mouth.
> (Proverbs 6:2 WEB)

> For by thy words thou shalt be justified,
> and by thy words thou shalt be condemned.
> (Matthew 12:37 KJV)

At first glance, or at least when I first read it, most might apply that verse to after you are dead and in front of our creator. But right now, yes right now, you are being justified or condemned by the words spoken over your life. You're either free or in bondage by your words or the words of who you listen to. Are you going to listen to and repeat the words of CNN or the enemy that it's impossible for you that we should give up all hope? From back in the garden, it's always been who are you going to listen to? Satan tempted Eve by saying, "Has God really said?"

Just to add something very important here. I don't care if you have a "prophet of God," your pastor or whoever or an angel or some bright vision of light telling you to do something, if it is not in line with the Word of God, it's a lie. Some people feel like God was telling them to do this or that. I have heard stories of people telling of "God" telling them "healing" wasn't for them.

God and "his Word" are one. He *will not* tell you something opposite of what the Bible, "his Word," has already said! Period. God has promised us healing and so many other great and precious promises that can be proved by the Bible. Beware of liars and deceivers.

> For such men are false apostles, deceitful workers, masquerading as Christ's apostles. And no wonder, for even Satan masquerades as an angel of light. (2 Corinthians 11:13–14 WEB)

Remember this, and I don't care what it looks like. It's a lie that God doesn't want you healed. The biggest weapon the enemy has is deception and getting you to give up what's yours and accept his garbage. The devil only has to twist what you believe enough to make you ineffective. A Christian that is broke, sick, mad, bad, or sad is not going to be effective for the advancement of the kingdom. In the military, we always referred to the maximum effective range of a weapon. What is the maximum effective range of a defeated Christian? Zero! A big waste! I am speaking to myself as well. I want to be effective! If I'm stepping on your toes, it's okay, Jesus is the healer! We were made for so much more! If you accept the lies that the devil and the world are selling, you will never know how great your life can be and should be. When you get delivered and set free, you can help free others!

What lie from the enemy have you accepted? Did a little kid from your childhood call you "ugly" or "fat?" What lies are you saying about your life or things in your life? What have you accepted that someone else has told you that you couldn't do? What lie from the enemy have you repeated? Satan is not only a liar but a deceiver. He uses others to deceive, even family members. Do you know the difference between a liar and a deceiver? A deceiver may not know they are deceived or wrong. Have you ever fought over something and thought you were right but found out later you were totally wrong? Ask yourself this: Are you deceived about something, anything, or any area of your life?

Think about any area of life you are trying to improve or an area you've been getting your butt kicked. What has been said about it, especially by you? Example, "My boss is a jerk"; "So and so doesn't like me and is out to get me"; "It doesn't matter what I eat, I can't seem to lose weight"; "I am big-boned"; "I can't eat that because I'm allergic to it"; "I can't find a job because no one is hiring"; "All the men in my family die early from heart attacks, so I probably won't live to see fifty"; "I tried that, but it didn't work for me"; or "I can't do that." (I probably hear these last two the most, and if you say it, guess what, you're right.) Start listening to the words of your mouth and everyone around you, and you'll be amazed at what you hear. Our words are setting our boundaries and are limiting us, and yes, our words are killing us.

So how do we take back control of our lives and truly step into our God-given authority? Confession is made unto salvation Romans 10:10. Yes, confession always precedes salvation. What you are confessing determines if you are justified or condemned. So start with making sure you won't be condemned eternally. Start with the greatest confession.

The Greatest Confession

Confessing Jesus Christ as Lord!

Christianity has been called the great confession. All the promises of God are unlocked when you confess Jesus as Lord. You get eternal life not just in heaven but here on earth. You become a child of God, and "in Christ" is where your true authority is unlocked. And all the promises and power of God can be unleashed the way they are supposed to be. Many have accepted Jesus but are powerless because their words have remained unchanged, and they have spoken against God himself. So they say, "I tried that Christianity thing, and it doesn't work." One verse really sticks out to me about this. Jesus one time asked his disciples, "Who do you say I am?" (Matthew 16:13). We have what we say and who we say God is, and what he can do is important!

We have the power of God to benefit mankind (and yes, our own lives too) right here on earth. We don't have to wait to go to heaven. It's supposed to be like that here on earth the way God intended in the garden. God wants fellowship with us. God doesn't need us, but he wants us. God wants to show off to the world and to anyone who "doesn't know him." And we get that by what we confess. Testimonies are how we overcome evil, and it lets others know what is possible for them and shows them the "way."

> And they overcame him by the blood of
> the Lamb, and by the word of their testimony.
> (Revelation 12:11 KJV)

Just one testimony that I give lets you know that overcoming even the worst addiction is possible. Multiple lifelong addictions gone forever. The best present I ever gave myself (and continue to give myself) was thirty days of being sober for my forty-second birthday. September 2, 2012, was the last time I drank alcohol or took pain pills. If I can do it, then you can do it. Also faith comes by hearing "and hearing by the word of God" (Romans 10:17).

We unlock the forces of heaven by what we speak. When we speak life, life and light get released onto the scene (and the darkness can never extinguish it). When we speak death or corruption, then darkness is released on the scene. Did you know angels are waiting to "harken" unto you if you speak the right things?

Unemployed Angels

If you are a child of God, you have angels that are supposed to be working for you. Are they unemployed? Angels are waiting to hear and move and act on the spoken word of God.

> Are they not all ministering spirits, sent forth to minister for them who shall be heirs of salvation? (Hebrews 1:14 KJV)

Heirs of salvation that's me and you if Jesus is your Lord! Woo-hoo! I am in the army now, and I have backup! Yeah, buddy!

When you're on the playground and your big brother is with you, you feel invincible! Well, you should feel sassy cause you got your big brother, Jesus, and there are legions of angels waiting to enforce God's word in your life! Woo-hoo!

> Bless the Lord, ye his angels, that excel in strength, that do his commandments, hearkening unto the voice of his word. (Psalms 103:20 KJV)

It's up to us to give voice to the word of the Lord. We have angels (the army of heaven), waiting for us to confess and release the forces of God and heaven. But unfortunately, the majority of the children of God don't know that what they are saying is binding them from acting. They are complaining and saying why the enemy is winning. You even hear Christians "testify" more about how powerful the devil is or how it's hopeless in the world. Hurry up, Jesus, and come take me away. Yep, unemployed angels with nothing to do because the "wrong" things are being said. When we confess God's word over our lives, God and his angels will enforce it.

Put your angels to work!

Do you want to put your angels to work? Do you want to confirm and be sure you are a child of God and claim your inheritance?

Confessing Jesus, who is the living word, equals salvation.
The promise that unlocks all the other promises and the goodness of God…

> But what saith it? The word is nigh thee, even in thy mouth, and in thy heart: that is, the word of faith, which we preach; That if thou shalt confess with thy mouth the Lord Jesus, and shalt believe in thine heart that God hath raised him from the dead, thou shalt be saved. For with the heart man believeth unto righteousness; and *with the mouth confession is made unto salvation. (Romans 10:8–10 KJV)

> For all the promises of God in him are yea, and in him Amen, unto the glory of God by us. (2 Corinthians 1:20 KJV)

All of God's promises are yea and amen but are for those *in him*, yes only for God's children. To be a child of God and to receive everything your Heavenly Father has provided, you need Jesus as your savior. Oh, the wonderful word yes, that a child hears from their parent. And so wonderful when the child reaches for and calls out to the parent and their heart melts.

> But as many as received him, to them gave he power to become the sons of God, even to them that believe on his name. (John 1:12 KJV)

Young's Literal Translation says this:

> But as many as did receive him to them he gave authority to become sons of God—to those believing in his name. (John 1:12)

> For this is good and acceptable in the sight of God our Saviour; Who will have all men to be saved, and to come unto the knowledge of the truth. (1 Timothy 2:3–4 KJV)

God wants you saved! If you want the power and authority of being a child of God and all the rights that come with it, you have to accept Jesus as your Lord and Savior! If you have never asked Jesus into your heart, you can do that right now by confessing it out loud.

Ask Jesus into your heart prayer here (say it out loud):

Father, it is written in your Word that if I confess with my mouth that Jesus is Lord and believe in my heart that you have raised him from the dead, I shall be saved.

Therefore, Father, I confess that Jesus is my Lord. I make him the Lord of my life right now. I believe in my heart that you raised Jesus from the dead. I repent and turn from my old ways. I renounce Satan and close the door to any of his devices.

I thank you for forgiving me of all my sins. Jesus, I give you permission to be the Lord of my life and lead me by your spirit, which is now alive in me. I am a new creation. Old things have passed away; now all things are new in Jesus's name. Amen. (Confession based on Romans 10:9–10, 1 John 1:9, and 2 Corinthians 5:17)

If you just became aware of your need to accept Jesus and said the prayer above, "praise God." Oh, those burdens and weights that were just lifted. Praise God, and there is a party in heaven because of you!

Now, God will end your captivity and restore you and your fortunes! God has a plan for you and your life. God's plan is for you to have a future filled with hope.

Know this, God's plan and thoughts for you are *good*! (Jeremiah 29:11)

When I gave Jesus full permission to be my Lord again that's when the outcome of the battles in my life started to shift. God's blessing started to flow and change my life for the better. When I started seeking God out and planting his Word in my heart and starting speaking it over my life, I was completely transformed. It didn't happen overnight, but gradually every part of my life began to be filled with the blessing of God. My life became worth living. I am now prospering "like watered grass." There is good fruit to show what has been planted. I am harvesting good. In just the last six months to a year, my physical transformation has really transformed and manifested and really started to show for all the work I have been doing the last couple of years.

My consistency in word and action is paying off and showing physically in my body. Now that I'm under two hundred and my muscles are developing and becoming more defined, people are asking me what I'm doing? When the bad is stripped away from the good, it becomes visible to others. When you have good results show up in your life, people want to know what you're doing. This world is so hungry and wanting answers. They are so tired of what they are doing and not having it work for them. People want results, and you either have them or you don't. It makes sense to ask someone, who has what you want, how they got it.

So, how do you get there? If you looked at a map or an aerial view from above of where you wanted to go, first you would have to "see" or "become aware" of where you were at then look at and plan how to get where you want to go. If you had someone, who had been there before, that is even better. Well, guess what, I have been "there."

The "there" that is terrible and horrible. Let me share some of what has helped me the most to change my life for the better. Awareness is the first step because if you don't think you need to change, you won't.

Awareness Is the First Step to Making Change

The more I see and hear, the more I realize most people don't even recognize what words are coming out of their mouth. They aren't aware of a need to change how they speak. Most Christians don't even realize that it's their words that are preventing God from moving in their life. They are waiting on God, but he is waiting on them. Thank God, we in the United States, where I live, still have freedom of speech (at least we still do at the writing of this), but just because we can say whatever we want doesn't mean that we shouldn't choose our words wisely.

I have heard people say, yes friends say, "Well I just don't have a filter. I say whatever comes to my mind." We need to filter what we say. Our words are a matter of life and death. First, get death out of your mouth and "set a watch over your mouth." Make yourself become and remain "aware" of the words that are coming out of your mouth. Treat your words like bullets. Don't just fire your mouth off all willy-nilly. The words you are saying are creating and destroying. If you're old enough to remember, Smokey, the bear, said, "Only you can prevent forest fires."

Only you can prevent the fires created by your mouth.

> And the tongue is a fire, a world of iniquity: so is the tongue among our members, that it defileth the whole body, and setteth on fire

the course of nature; and it is set on fire of hell.
(James 3:6 KJV)

It's time to put out the fires you have been creating with your mouth!

Patterned Behavior and Changing Your Course

Have you ever been driving to do something else but were traveling on the route you take to work every day and without thinking miss your exit or go the wrong way because without thinking you stayed in your normal daily pattern? This has happened to me several times like the time Owen didn't have school, and I was supposed to take him over to his mom's. And I missed the exit because my routine was taking him to school. Patterned behavior is powerful and takes real conscious effort to change.

Even when you become aware that your words matter, it requires changing what is called patterned behavior. You have to change your bad habits. It is a deliberate choice and has taken much effort on my part to change my pattern of behavior to not say something that is funny but harmful to me or not something to get sympathy from someone. I may want to say it, but if it is not what I want or want to get more of, I leave it unsaid. Patterned behavior or habitual behavior is so powerful. I one time rearranged the kitchen in my house at the time and moved the garbage can from the end of the counter to the other side of the room over by the fridge. Do you know how many times I walked to the end of the glorious counter to throw something away? (At the time I wouldn't have used a nice word here as at the time I wasn't speaking and walking in saving words.)

Why did I walk to the end of the counter? I was the one who moved the garbage can! I know where I put it. When you want to change something, especially if it's part of your everyday life, you have to basically reprogram yourself. As with diet and exercise, regular behavior has to become regular or made part of your "new" pattern. Doing something consistently for about a month will make it the new normal and easier to do without thinking about it so much. You can find someone that is doing and getting the results that you want and copy them. Make their habits yours. Being around others can work for you or against you. Most likely, the ones you are currently around are doing the same bad things you are and enabling you, or they are supporting what you do or, even worse, encouraging you to do the bad things they are doing.

Remember the pot. Get out of the pot, and don't let your crabby friends pull you down. If you are around someone that does what you used to, you still have to fight the temptation of falling back into your old routine or pattern. It's an easy path. It's easier to do what you have always done than do something new. Remember the first time driving or doing something difficult. Your unconscious mind makes your life easier, so you don't have to think about all the routine and repetitive tasks that you do every day and frees up your mind to think about other things. Your unconscious mind (the decisions that are made seemingly without "thinking" or how your unconscious mind works) is like the woods. You have paths that are already created, but they will always lead to the same places.

So if you want to go somewhere new or if you want to change and go a different direction, even if it's only slightly different, you have to blaze a new trail, and that is where the work is required. You have to clear the brush, chop down trees and brush, and hack limbs and branches and tall grass out of your way. You have to reprogram or "rewire" your brain. A short side note here if you keep traveling the same path and get bit by a snake every time you go down that path, wouldn't you stop going down that path? Alcohol for me was that path, so I quit going down that path. Do you keep going down the same path? Ice cream or food you can't resist. Fights with a loved one. If you don't like where you are at and where you keep ending up, change your path, and start that by changing your words.

Words that come out of the heart bypass the mind and your thinking, so a lot of what you say you may not even be aware of.

Say this now out loud, "I command myself to become aware of all my words. I am aware of my words, and I am consciously aware of what I am saying in relation to what I am getting."

As words come out of your mouth, I want you to consciously think about what direction are your words going? Are your words describing what you want or where you want to be? If the answer is no, stop speaking that. It's by your words that you change your direction and outcome.

Your Mouth Is the Steering Wheel!

What comes to mind if our mouth is the steering wheel? I hear the line from that popular Carrie Underwood song, "Jesus, Take The Wheel."

Set a watch, O LORD, before my mouth; keep the door of my lips (Psalm 141:3 KJV).

Your words and mouth control your direction, where you are looking, and ultimately where you are going.

What is your focus? Your mind is like the sight of a gun, and your mouth releases the bullets. Anyone who is an expert with any weapon knows that your sight picture is the most important part of hitting your target. If you are looking at the wrong thing, your bullet will not only not hit the target or backstop but may end up "way off in the weeds" or worse "hit an innocent bystander." So wherever your focus is, it is of vital importance. Also, whatever you focus on you will get more of.

Our minds tend to notice what is important to us. Have you ever bought a new car that you may have never seen before, but once you bought it, you see them everywhere even the same color just like yours? They were already there, but your mind is now seeing them because they are now part of your awareness. What are your words focusing on? Positive or negative? Are you focusing on what you want or what makes you upset? This is critical because whatever you are focusing on, you will see more of. If it is something you *do not* want, then *stop* focusing on that and *stop* speaking about it.

Get your focus on what you want, and start saying you *have* what you want. That it always happens that way. This is going to take some time to change the course of what may already be a lifelong pattern for you, but *start now!* The journey of a thousand steps starts with the first step. Get in the habit of looking for and catching your kids doing good, and reward them for it by telling them "thank you" or doing something special for them. It's too easy to pick out people's shortcomings. There may be many things wrong in this world, and yes, there is evil. But you don't have to go that way. Your body, your car, and your bike are all designed to go the direction you are looking.

Start now and decide to change your direction, decide to change your focus, change where you are looking to, and change the words that come out of your mouth.

> Indeed, we put bits into the horses' mouths so that they may obey us, and we guide their whole body. Behold, the ships also, though they are so big and are driven by fierce winds, are yet guided by a very small rudder, wherever the pilot desires. (James 3:3–4 WEB)

James, here in the Bible, through the Holy Spirit, tells us that your tongue is what you use to steer where you are going. James used the examples of a bit in a horse's mouth and the rudder on a ship. Both the bit and the rudder are very small in comparison to the size of the vessel, but they control the "body." The rudder seems so small to the size of the ship, and yet, the captain uses that to maneuver whichever way he wants to go. You are the captain of your ship. No matter how terrible the storm, your tongue will steer you. You are in authority as long as you are in control. Regardless of your situation, you can change the course of where you are going.

In this case, the deciding factor is your tongue. Are you in control of your words? Are you conscious of the words you are using? If James wrote today, he would probably use the example of your tongue as the steering wheel in a car. You are the driver on the road of life, and you hold the steering wheel. Which way are you going? Are you where you want to be? Are you even headed in the right direction? Even a slow-moving turtle will eventually get to their destination if pointed the right way. If you were on a road headed to a city and you never got there at some point, you would realize the need to change direction or try a different road or get a new map. If you are not where you want to be, *you* have to make a change.

For a good change, focus on the positive. Most people focus on the things wrong, and that's how they pray. Don't tell God about your problems. When you're confessing them is not when he found out about them. He already knew about them before you had them. Talk to your problems about your God! Tell whatever it is, that is going wrong, to "stop it." "Devil, you are defeated! My God is greater than 'this situation.' My God will deliver me! I don't know how, but he will find a way! I know he'll come by it honestly." Say anything good, but don't say, "There is no way." Without going into all the details, just very recently, we had a financial thing, and my wife said to me twice after going over the numbers, "There is no way."

To add here, I thought the very same thing or feared the same thing, but I said, "Wait let's not say that. There is a way, and God is the way." So I was praying about it and working on not letting fear and doubt creep in. So I said to myself, "If I really believed it, what would I say?" So I spoke out loud and claimed it as mine and claimed what I needed and all the resources to do it in the name of Jesus. The answers with the resources came within two to three hours. When it was all said and done, we ended up having ten times what we needed.

It went from being out of the question to not even being a question. Every situation is different, and when you get the outcome varies. But you keep your words right, and you hold onto faith in God. Now finances for me have been where I have had to really build my faith. When I was little, we were poor. Poor mouthed is what I should call it. "We can't afford that?"; "We're broke"; "Robbing Peter to Pay Paul!"; etc. were phrases I heard on a regular basis.

Are you fat? You got a fat mouth! I know I did. Changing your words changes everything. Everyone is going to have an area where they have to work harder on steering their mouth in the right direction. Maybe money has never been an issue in your family, but health problems run rampant in your family. Maybe everyone in your family is overweight. The key here is keeping your focus and words right and calling into existence the very thing you don't have but need.

Calling the Dog

How to acquire provision in your new kingdom as a child of God? Remember you are a king and what you say goes. We are to act like our father, "who calls those things that be not as though they were."

> (As it is written, I have made thee a father of many nations,) before him whom he believed, even God, who quickeneth the dead, and calleth those things which be not as though they were. (Romans 4:17 KJV)

The World English Bible says it like this:

> As it is written, "I have made you a father of many nations." This is in the presence of him whom he believed: God, who gives life to the dead, and calls the things that are not, as though they were. (Romans 4:17)

Whoa! God gives life to dead things! That verse gets me excited! God did that for me! God brought my dead carcass back to life! Woo-hoo!

Calling those things that be not as though they were!

This is a foundational Bible principle. God calls those things that "be not" or "are not" as though "they were." He summons the things that do not yet exist as though they do. The cat may be licking you in your face, but you don't call the cat when you want the dog. You never call the cat when you want the dog. You call the dog till he comes. This is a biblical principle to call things that be not as though they were. You don't speak lack when you want abundance. You don't speak sickness when you want health. When you pray, you have to say and believe that you have received it already.

> Therefore I tell you, all things whatever you pray and ask for, believe that you have received them, and you shall have them. (Mark 11:24 WEB)

You have to believe you have already received it *when* you pray. Your first step of believing that you have received is with your words. Faith is always present tense. Now, faith is (Hebrews 11:1). So I confess what I have (it may not be visible yet). I have healing; it's mine. Jesus bought and paid for it over two thousand years ago. By his stripes, I *am* healed (Isaiah 53:5). By whose stripes ye (yes, you too) were healed (1 Peter 2:24). If I were healed, then I *am* healed. I don't have to *try* to get it! Healing's already *mine*! I have it! I say it! And I act like it! I walk by faith and not by sight (2 Corinthians 5:7), or I don't walk by feelings either.

On this note, the devil can control your outside world and what you perceive with the five senses, so you have to override him and not give up easily. This is the only fight we have, the good fight of faith (1 Timothy 6:12), and this is *how* we please God. For it is impossible to please God without faith (Hebrews 11:6). Remember faith is what is in your heart and what you confess with your mouth. When I had hurt my knee back in about 2014, I really got serious about divine healing. I needed my knee healed, and I couldn't hardly walk. I had been severely injured before, and I know how it works with a bunch of time in physical therapy and surgery. Lots of time and money I didn't want to deal with. I praise God for people like my PT guys from the past, Craig and Michael, from Spokane Sports and Physical Therapy.

They can personally witness how messed up I was before my healing. So this is probably when I first started learning about "healing scriptures" and was listening to Kenneth Hagin's "God's medicine." Great compilation of scriptures to listen to for receiving and getting healing planted in you, and by the way, you can find it on YouTube. So I was pouring healing scriptures into me every chance I got and was speaking life over my knee. I was speaking things that were not as though they were. I was calling my knee "strong" when it "hurt" and "was weak." One thing that I decided or was somehow led by the spirit was about my communication. I had heard this verse in the King James Version, and the first part of the verse jumped out at me about effective communication of faith.

Effectual Communication of Faith

That the communication of thy faith may become effectual by the acknowledging of every good thing which is in you in Christ Jesus. (Philemon 1:6 KJV)

So this just kept churning over and over in my spirit about the communication of my faith being effectual. Communication is more than words. I learned, when I worked as a correctional officer and being a tactical verbal instructor, that nonverbal communication is more important than words sometimes. Actions speak louder than words. Faith without works is dead (James 2:17). Or a more accurate or understandable interpretation would be faith without corresponding action is dead. Mind you, I couldn't hardly walk or do stairs. I decided for me to do my best in every way to not communicate my pain physically or otherwise or call my knee "my bad knee."

In addition to speaking to my knee calling it strong. I would exercise and do what I could, and if I did a squat or took a step and my knee hurt, I would say, "Thank you" instead of "ouch." "I would thank God and be thankful for whatever it was that I could do even if it hurt." Be thankful for what you have, and God will give you more. You have to act doing what you can and do things "as if" you were healed. Do something even if it seems a waste. It's the acting and movement in belief that opens the door. When you go to the grocery store, most stores have doors that have a little sensor that will open the door for you.

You could stand back a certain distance from the door and say the door is shut. That's what most people do concerning faith. They keep saying and acting as if the door is shut. The door won't open until you move toward it and get close to it. That is how faith works. You say and act as if. If I am healed, I am working out, walking, and doing stairs straight on. I would do what I could do, and then I started to be able to do more. Being thankful all the way. I would say things like I have extra cushion in my knees (now I say all my joints) and strong connective tissue in my body. I have added now that I have full range of motion in my body with no pain or swelling.

It took six months, and my knee was totally healed. You might say, "Well, you could have done that with PT." Maybe, maybe not. Six to nine months is the short end of injuries like that but at $50 a pop, which I just checked is what I would have to pay *with* insurance and at two to three times a week. The point here is that not all divine healing is someone laying their hands on you and you are instantly healed. I have had that work through me, but you can't control that. As you grow in your knowledge of God, his word is required more. The more you know, the more is required of you. *Faith in the word will work a hundred percent of the time if you don't give up.*

Now this is another point I have to bring up, that after that, my knee would only hurt when it made sense. If I jumped up and down during praise and worship or bowling, etc. I then heard this phrase, and this is really important, "If it makes sense, then it probably doesn't make faith, and if it makes faith, it probably doesn't make sense." It makes no sense for a woman to have a child never knowing a man, but Mary said, "Be it unto me." Wow! World-changing faith. So I had to say, "No!" Doesn't matter how much I jump up and down or how much I weighed at the time I confessed "my knee is healed, in Jesus's name!" By his stripes, I *am* healed (Isaiah 53:5)! So my knee is completely healed and thus began my victory over physical defeat and my journey seeking and learning all I could about learning and using God's word and my words to be healed and whole in every way and praying and speaking God's word over every area of my life.

Getting Your "But" in the Right Place!

Inevitably once you set out to control your words, someone asks, "How you are doing?" And you may be in the middle of a "shit storm" or you're hurting so bad, it would be easier to fall down than to continue standing, and I have been there. But you now know your words matter and that you have to say the right things. The word but is a connecting word, but (see there it is) it negates or restricts what was said before it. If I said to you, "That's a nice haircut you got, but it makes your ears look big." You wouldn't take it as a compliment even though I said it was nice. Make sure you get "your but" in the right place and use it for good.

Example, I feel sick, but the word of God says by his stripes I *am healed* (1 Peter 2:24 and Isaiah 53:5). If I said the opposite, it would negate what God has said, and I would be saying or agreeing that sickness or Satan has more power than God. You may be feeling the fact of sickness in your body, but by agreeing with the ultimate truth and getting your words right, you will conquer the situation. I don't deny there are germs, sickness, etc., but I deny their right to me because Jesus removed them from me and "all the things wrong with me."

Jesus bought and paid for my freedom! I am redeemed, and I say so! So let's do another example. "If you were to ask my throat, if it was healed, it would say no. The question was if you were to ask my throat, or have it say if it sounds better, "my throat would say no." If I was to ask you if I sound healed, you would say no, but I believe God and God's word says I am healed. God sent his word and healed

64

me, and by the blood and stripes of Jesus, "I am healed!" I actually saw a good example of getting your but in the wrong place on a sign (the writing of this book during the "Covid pandemic, lies, and more deception from the enemy"). "Trust God, but wear a mask." The sign should have said, "Wear a mask, but trust God." Do you see the difference? Do you see where the "trust" is? Do you see where the devil or your thoughts could allow you to "get sick."

Now I will put on a mask for making others feel better or if required, but I am vocal about where my trust is if anyone asks. I thank God that I don't have to trust in the failing devices of this world and I cannot imagine having to go through life these days without God. My trust will never be in a mask, vaccine, or anything of this world! If anything negative like that hits me, it would still be in my mouth that it is God that delivers me. Now I have been saying, "By his stripes I am healed," for quite some time now. I have been living in divine health for many years now. The battles will come, but God is the deliverer. As you get better and grow in faith, you will get better faster and get sick less and less. The more of God's word you get into your heart, the stronger and healthier you'll be. Start planting health in your body now for a healthy tomorrow! What you believe and say today will affect what you say and believe tomorrow, so *start today*!

Part of getting what you say right is preparing in advance! In martial arts and in the military, we would practice over and over how to respond to different types of attacks from the enemy so when it happened you just responded automatically without having to think about it. Remember the woods. Create the right paths before the attack comes. When I worked in corrections, you would go over and over "what if such and such happens," so if it did, you already knew what you were going to do. Know what you are going to say about something if someone asks you. Ask yourself, "If I really believe this and have this, what would I say about it?"

Remember when I said I had been in a place where it would be easier to fall down than to stand. In a situation I will go over more later on counterattacks, I was dealing with pain and physical weakness. I had determined no matter how bad it got, if anyone asked me "how I was," I was going to say, "I am strong in the Lord and in the power of his might!" There was a bunch of scriptures on strength I was quoting daily and even hourly when I needed it, but my short answer was strong in the Lord or strong in the Lord and in the power of his might.

I remember numerous times being asked even by my pastor how I was doing. So I said I was strong until I was. Didn't matter how hurt or weak I felt, I responded with, "I am strong." "Let the weak say I am strong" (Joel 3:10). That's how it works. So prepare in advance and remain steadfast that you already have what you need, and make sure your response is right. It's just like gardening or farming when you have planted the seed, but you can't "see" anything happening. You have it; you just can't see the results yet, but by keeping the faith, you will see it come to fruition. Don't worry about failing. Fail fast and forward. If you fall, just pick yourself up, dust yourself off, and keep moving forward. Never quit; remember what I said in the beginning of the book, it's not three strikes and you're out. You play until you win!

Being Specific to Be Terrific!

I don't remember where I got this phrase, but I really like it. And it works well—you have to be specific to be terrific! Without going in too deep on how to get results in prayer, as that is a book in itself, your prayer and words must be based on the word of God. When I pray, I base my prayers on multiple verses, but the main scripture is Mark 11:22–24, having what you say and believing you have received. Then with what I say, I am being specific to be terrific. Note if you aren't specific, how will you know if your prayer got answered?

General efforts get general results. So when I pray, I just say what I want to happen. I speak the desired outcome. I am not merely begging or asking God for it from a position of weakness. I am taking my God-given authority and dominion that Jesus won back for us. I command what I want to happen. Side note: You don't have to "pray" it, but you do have to "say" it, if you pray it. When I pray, I am taking the authority God has given me, and I am commanding in Jesus's name (John 14:13) and or confessing that we have received it already (believing that you have received; Mark 11:24), and the testimonies I have are awesome! Praise God!

One time, when we needed my mom's house to sell urgently, the story goes like this, we had a buyer, and the deal fell through at the last minute. And we really needed it sold, but we hadn't had any action on the house since the first offer. The time crunch for us to sell and get the money we needed to get mom into a good-assisted living place, was so short, and it looked impossible. Had to be that week or something like that. I was leaving her house and stopped the car just out of the driveway and got my youngest, who was in the car with me out. When you live by faith and walk in authority, having witnesses is great, and teaching your children is even better.

So, I told Owen to point at the house with me and command it to sell in Jesus's name, and I threw in that we would have a buyer by Saturday (specific). Long story short, we got the offer we needed, and it sold! There was even a situation when doing the paperwork that I had to call in the title "found" that day, and it happened. And I told everyone "my testimony," who would listen, the guy who did the title paperwork, and so on. Everyone that knows me knows how "awesome *my* God is!"

Start writing down your prayers, and keep track of who you pray for and the results. I have gone back to notebooks I have kept from back to 2012. I have gone back and read and said, "Wow, I forgot about that! God answered that prayer that I thought that was impossible!" You may be up against something you're feeling is just too big right now when he has already done something even bigger that you forgot about. And something to note here, the devil will really downplay what God has done in your life. Revisit what God has already done for you, and it will pump you up and build your faith for even greater signs and wonders to take place in your life.

Being Selective to Be Effective! Rejecting What Is Not For Us!

If someone dropped a package at your door that was full of venomous snakes, you wouldn't "accept it" and bring it into your house. You would reject it and send it back. You definitely wouldn't bring it into your house unless you're a weirdo. Don't accept anything bad as final, period! Sickness is not for us. Jesus was sent to destroy the works of the devil (1 John 3:8).

> How God anointed Jesus of Nazareth with the Holy Ghost and with power: who went about doing good, and healing all that were oppressed of the devil; for God was with him. (Acts 10:38 KJV)

Sickness is "fathered" by and "is" demonic or satanic oppression. It is *not* from God. It is not for you, and you should reject it. I hear people all the time saying, "My diabetes, my cancer, or my glaucoma." It's not yours. When you say it's yours, you take ownership. Doctors are great, and most doctor's advice should be followed (if you question [if there is *any* question by you] whether you should seek medical help, "*get it*"), but when they say there is nothing they can do or there is no hope no cure or "they say" you got to die, reject that! Period. This is where faith can show up so glorious because that is when people have no other choice but to depend on God.

My friend Pat got a bad report from his doctor. Pat was told by his surgeon, when he had a brain tumor, that no one ever survives this type of cancer even with aggressive treatment. Pat and his wife,

Mary, were told to prepare for the various stages of grief and anger. They were told he had about six months give or take maybe longer with multiple surgeries to keep removing the cancer. Pat and Mary decided to *not* receive the doctor's "words" as final but decided rather to stand on God's word that "by his stripes we are healed."

They continued to reject the doctor's report and confess Pat's complete healing. There is obviously more to the story, but the main point I want to convey is that, Pat rejected that "he had to die" that "no one ever survives this" from this guy who is the "expert" on the subject who was a real brain surgeon. It was no laughing matter. The reports said he was as good as dead, and it was a done deal. Pat got into the word and read and listened to healing scriptures and confessed God's word over his life. Pat's wife, Mary, equally rejected the prognosis. Mary tells of waking one night to a flood of doubt and questions and whispers of the enemy that maybe the naysayers are right.

What if Pat dies? She feels compelled to check their insurance policies. This is when it matters. She stops and says—and this is the kicker—what you say and receive matters, Mary said, "Wait a minute devil. You are a liar! My husband will live and not die, in the name of Jesus Christ!" They both rejected the doctor's report like I did and then got in the word of God and received God's healing that he has already provided for everyone. And continually he said, and this is the most important part, he was healed even before he actually had any evidence to say otherwise. Pat is healed and whole now. Pat has been living cancer-free for over six years now.

I have another friend, Mike, who also got a bad medical report. My friend Mike's wife was told her husband could probably die, and the chances were high. And if the surgery was successful, he would still never be "the same" again. She as Mike puts it, "Patty politely refused to receive that." Mike, before he went into surgery, prayed in front of all the medical staff that were present right before they started the surgery by publicly confessing and rejecting that he was going to die. He said, "I shall not die but live and declare the works of God" (Psalm 118:17).

At this point, this is the beforehand part of "our testimony" like David, against Goliath, proclaimed the outcome before the battle. The hardest part of the battle is in the mind and listening to the lies of the enemy. Don't accept the situation as final. Yes, the situation may seem like an immovable or undefeatable giant, but you have to "say it!" You have to speak to every mountain in your way. Speak and command "that mountain to be lifted up and thrown into the sea" (and for good measure, I would add "return no more"). So not only did Mike get through the surgery, but he has been fully restored, healed, back to work, and back to normal.

Not some new lesser normal or worse situation, but Mike was healed. Mike and Pat declared they were healed and not going to die based on God's word for us. And that's how I did it as well. I spoke to every part of my body that was broken. Many have thought it was the "will of God" for them to live in poverty or to "be sick," and many have died believing that. More lies of the enemy. God has already given you the answer and the authority to change any attack of the enemy or anything that is not beneficial to you. Do not receive the attack or anything that is not of God. Just like you can't put everything in your house in your mouth, as some of the stuff under the sink could kill you. Be selective; filter out what is not for you. Once you decide what is not for you, then you have to speak against them and *all* the lies of the enemy, and "bind," "reject," and "forbid" their presence in your life.

Authority Is Yours! You "Have" the Keys to the Kingdom!

> And I will give unto thee the keys of the kingdom of heaven: and whatsoever thou shalt bind on earth shall be bound in heaven: and whatsoever thou shalt loose on earth shall be loosed in heaven. (Matthew 16:19 KJV)

In one translation, the word *keys* translates into the word *authority*. The keys to your success are using your authority to bind and loose. The word bind also translates to whatever you forbid or declare to be unlawful or improper. The word loose also translates to whatever you permit or allow or declare to be lawful or proper. If you look up the biblical meaning online, it says bind means to forbid by indisputable authority, and loose means permit or allow by indisputable authority.

So whatever you allow or permit will be allowed. Whatever you forbid will be forbidden on earth and in heaven. Heaven will allow what you allow. You're the king, and what you say goes!

Your power and authority come from heaven. The power is already there, but the "light switch" to release the power requires you and you using the authority God has given you. You wouldn't ask the power company to turn on your lights. You're connected; you have the power and authority to light your house, but you have to flip the switch. You could sit in the dark if you want to.

So we have the power to bind or loose, but we have to do it with our words.

So execution looks something like this, "strife you are forbidden from my house, and I will not permit you. I bind you in Jesus's name and forbid you from operating against me and my family. You are loosed from your assignment against us!" or "cancer you are loosed from your assignment against me. I bind you from operating against me, and I forbid you from existing in my body. I call you gone in Jesus's name!"

What are you allowing in your life that is bringing discomfort, distress, or disease? Start binding and loosing what needs to be bound or loosed. What are you permitting or allowing in your life that sucks? You have to take your God-given authority and use it. You have to speak against the forces of evil and, like David, run at your giant telling it where to go—"Go back to the pit of hell where you came from! I am going to cut your head off. My God is going to deliver me!" When you proclaim that your God is greater, you give your angels and God the ability to act on your behalf. You have to treat whatever is trying to come against you like the stray that comes in your yard to "crap" in your territory. With every fiber of your body fiercely demanding, "You get! Go on! Get out of *here*! Devil, get your junk and get out of here and return no more!" This is no time to be polite especially when it's life and death on the line. This is how we fight our battles. This is how we defeat our enemies. Our God has given us everything we need for living a godly life! But we have to soldier up and fight the enemy, and we do it with our mouth and words.

Whatever the enemy has plotted, planned, or schemed that is against the Lord, he will bring to an end. The enemy will be destroyed and shall not rise up a second time.

> What do ye imagine against the Lord? He
> will make an utter end: affliction shall not rise up
> the second time. (Nahum 1:9 KJV)

When faced with an impossible situation, see what God has to say about it. That is why you will see and "hear" me say and quote so much of God's word for three reasons specifically. (1) In Psalms 91:4 it says, "His truth shall be thy shield and buckler." Yes, God's word, his truth, his word is my armor, my protection, and my defense, so I speak "his Word" why? (2) Because God's word "never returns void or empty or without any effect" (Isa. 55:11). (3) "He watches over his word to perform it" (Jer. 1:12). If you want real weapons and protection, come in agreement with, and say what God says. And then he will fulfill it in your life.

Find the promise of God for your situation and confess that it's yours, for his words never return void or empty.

> So shall my word be that goeth forth out
> of my mouth: it shall not return unto me void,
> but it shall accomplish that which I please, and
> it shall prosper in the thing whereto I sent it.
> (Isaiah 55:11 KJV)

God intends his word to be fulfilled and prosper in the thing where he sent it, and it never returns without effect. Well, guess what? He sent his Word "to us" and "healed us!" (Psalms 107:20)

> He sent his word, and healed them, and
> delivered them from their destructions. (Psalms
> 107:20 KJV)

> Beloved, I wish above all things that thou
> mayest prosper and be in health, even as thy soul
> prospereth. (3 John 1:2 KJV)

God will step over a thousand million people to get to and show himself strong to the one of faith.

For the eyes of the Lord run to and fro throughout the whole earth, to shew himself strong in the behalf of them whose heart is perfect toward him. (2 Chronicles 16:9 KJV)

How do we get our heart perfect toward him? Easy, fill your heart with his Word. And we fill our hearts by speaking. *So, speaking God's word is the number one way to heal what ails you and the number one way to life and life more abundant.*

When I first was looking for healing (for every part of me), I found God. Thank God the seeds were planted. Seeds I don't even remember when I was little and the prayers of my mother and probably others. For the first time in my life, God was real—real to me. It was like he showed up strong and rescued me. Now, he was and has always been there, but I didn't "fellowship" with and know him. And my words were definitely "against" him. When I look back, I can see that now, that "he has never left me nor forsaken me" (Hebrews 13:5). "My eyes were blinded" (1 Corinthians 4:4) when I "was in my destructions" (Psalm 107:20), but now I see God has always been there with a desire to have a relationship with *me* and for me to have a rich, satisfying life.

God is no respecter of persons. What God does for one, he will do for another. What God has done for me, he'll do for you! God *loves* you and wants to have a relationship with *you* and for you to have a rich, satisfying life, and you can't have that if you're broken physically, spiritually, emotionally, or financially. This is where Christians get it *wrong. You are an example of the God you serve. What testimony is it for you to be defeated in any way. God doesn't miss it; we do.* Ask God to show you where you are missing it. The world should desire what we have. It's a lie that we have to wait to get to heaven before we get what God has provided for us. It's time to claim what is rightfully yours. It's time to claim "your" inheritance!

Claiming Your Inheritance!

> If you are Christ's, then you are Abraham's
> offspring and heirs according to promise.
> (Galatians 3:29 WEB)

That's right, if you belong to Christ, you're an heir to the promises. "Our inheritance," yes, "God's promises" are not just for when we get to heaven, but they are for here and now to save us and proclaim and show "who he is" and "how great and mighty our God is!"

It's not what you think or what man thinks or what this world thinks that is going to save you. Receiving what is ours as children of God is our "salvation," and it's our inheritance. Naturally, every father and parent wants what is best for their child. We want what is best for our children and so does our Father, God. If you had a really rich father who died, and he left you in "his will" not only would he want to make sure you got what he had that was yours but you as the recipient you also would definitely want to know and get what was left for you. God wants to make sure that you get what he has already provided for you, and he left "his instructions," "his word," and "his will." The Bible—and I love this, I got this from my son, Owen—means Basic Instructions Before Leaving Earth. The Bible, the Word of God, is God's will for our lives. It's more than just what we need to do before we leave earth, it's what we need to *know* and *say*, *do* and *have while we are here!* It's our inheritance!

God's word is full of his promises to us.

When we hold onto his word and hold onto his promises, God will manifest himself to us. God will not only manifest himself to us but he will come live with us.

> Judas saith unto him, not Iscariot, Lord, how is it that thou wilt manifest thyself unto us, and not unto the world? Jesus answered and said unto him, If a man love me, he will keep my words: and my Father will love him, and we will come unto him, and make our abode with him. (John 14:22–23 KJV)

Not only is God's word how he manifests himself to us but his word is how we observe or "see" what to do and how we can be prosperous and successful in all we do and so that we are able to deal wisely in the affairs of this life.

> This book of the law shall not depart out of thy mouth; but thou shalt meditate therein day and night, that thou mayest observe to do according to all that is written therein: for then thou shalt make thy way prosperous, and then thou shalt have good success. (Joshua 1:8 KJV)

For the definition of the word, meditate the strong's concordance uses words like mutter, ponder, imagine, utter, study, and talk. That is exactly what we are to do with God's word for success in our lives. I am living proof it works. My life is not recognizable now compared to where I was in my brokenness. I am a completely different person or as the word says a "new creation."

Confessing God's word over your situation is so important like many of the examples I have shared or the examples of Pat and Mike, both of them and their wives. They had confessed God's word and his promises over their situations and chose to believe that over everything else. Just like I did, they experienced God's deliverance and salvation. When you give God's word first place, it brings health to *all* your flesh (Proverbs 4:22)

In the middle of the crisis is not the time to go see what God has said. You have to have it planted firmly in your heart so it comes out with force and faith—faith in his word. Faith requires knowledge.

My people perish for a lack of knowledge!
(Hosea 4:6)

Remember that claiming your inheritance is knowing it's yours! It actually goes beyond that and when you get it past your head knowledge, but get it deep down on the inside of you that's when it will start to show. This is where you know that you know it's yours. I have so many examples of me personally or someone I know using God's word over a situation to be victorious and overcome what looked like imminent defeat. One of my favorite stories for claiming your inheritance based on the word of God is one that my pastor lived out.

It was during one of the fire seasons that was pretty bad in our area (which has led me to speak against them). My pastor's house was in an area where the fire was advancing toward their property. The fire department had shown up telling them to be ready to leave at a moment's notice. Then it happened that everyone was told to evacuate. As they looked back from down at the bottom of their hill, all the families watched as the fire raced up their hillside. My pastor who "is" a "tither" (Malachi 3:10) boldly pointed in the direction of his home, and he said, "The devourer is rebuked!"(Malachi 3:11). And he kept saying it.

When it was all said and done! There was almost a perfect circle around his property where the fire had stopped. On the edge of his property, only his tree's outer edges and leaves were scorched. One of his closest neighbors, whose door was only about seventy-five or a hundred feet or less from his doorstep, burnt completely to the ground. The wiring of the house, the glass, and the metal in the tires of their vehicle completely melted. The beginning temperature of where glass starts to melt is approximately 1,400 to 1,600 degrees. To say the fire was hot and would burn up anything in its path is an understatement. It was a little "hell" on earth that day. When everyone else says, "Oh, we could lose everything" or worse "No, we're going to lose everything!"

You say, "No, THE DEVOURER IS REBUKED! In Jesus's name!" My God has promised me that the devourer is rebuked!

Look closely at the verse my pastor was standing on, and you can then do the same!

> Bring ye all the tithes into the storehouse, that there may be meat in mine house, and prove me now herewith, saith the Lord of hosts, if I will not open you the windows of heaven, and pour you out a blessing, that there shall not be room enough to receive it. And I will rebuke the devourer for your sakes, and he shall not destroy the fruits of your ground; neither shall your vine cast her fruit before the time in the field, saith the Lord of hosts. And all nations shall call you blessed: for ye shall be a delightsome land, saith the Lord of hosts. (Malachi 3:10–12 KJV)

When you confess and act on the Word of God, everyone will call you blessed, and you won't be able to contain the blessing because it is so great. And the devourer won't ruin the fruits of your labor.

Counterattacks of the Enemy

Speaking of the devourer. Be prepared for a counterattack! They are a part of war! So be ready.

Remember again about the time I said it would be easier to fall than to stand.

> Put on the whole armour of God, that ye may be able to stand against the wiles of the devil. (Ephesians 6:11 KJV)

It goes on to say and I am going to paraphrase here, after you have done all you can to stand, just remain standing. Don't give up. I was going through a counterattack! Counterattacks from the enemy are where most battles are lost. You thought you won, and then bam, you're being hit again. You'll be confused and dazed. I am telling you this so you'll know what to expect. The best self-defense classes teach you exactly what to expect so you don't freeze or be taken over by fear. The thoughts you'll have will be like, *Well, I guess I didn't get it. I thought God healed me, but I guess I was wrong? Maybe God wants to teach me something? Did I do something wrong? Why does it seem like everyone gets it so easy but not me? Why is this so hard? Chuck always gets blessed, but I never get anything good!*

Whatever you do, scratch these types of phrases forever from your vocabulary! *Do not* open your mouth and give birth or life to these thoughts. Let them die aborted in your mind! Don't say or speak anything that the devil can capitalize on. In the army, we had to practice what we called noise discipline. Don't let the enemy hear you. Especially if you're hurting and wounded. That's when they come in for the kill to finish you off. And don't let negative thoughts run unrestrained and on replay loop in your head either. No one else may hear them, but you do. And your heart is connected to what you hear.

Remember, fear and faith both come by hearing. Don't ask questions that can allow the devil to come in because "you have opened the door." I remember hearing someone that I work with say, "Am I allergic to that?" The devil is always going to say, "Yes!" Back to the counterattack that was on me. This happened to me a little over a year ago, and I know I went through more than I had to because my words weren't right. I was going through the ringer! I was being attacked on every front. I had pain and symptoms in almost every area of my body. I later remember saying that I felt like every symptom or injury that I ever had has come back on me, then all hell broke loose.

I had opened the door to the enemy and let him in to wreak havoc. The enemy knew if he could defeat me here that he would prevent me from my destiny. And let me tell you brother, he was pouring it on, and I had opened the door *wide* for him to come in. I knew I was called to equip others to fight and train them how to be victorious and to walk in the power God has given us. If you have knowledge on how to do something, you should help others with it especially if you can see them struggling. If you know your ABCs, you can teach ABCs to those who don't. If you know how to tie your shoes, you can teach someone who doesn't. If you have over-come something, share it to encourage others, and help anyone that is going through what you went through.

So, I had had major verified victories in every area of my life, but if any of it didn't work for me, how could I tell you it will work for you? I think that is where most people give up. They have a cold or something or some small symptom, and they think well this faith stuff doesn't work. And what they think comes out their mouth, and they get what they say. They have some small defeat that then turns into the enemy running all over them in *every* area of their life. Remember this, even the greatest warriors with great victories can be brought down without their armor on or without their sword. The good fight of faith is the only fight we are called to fight. You can't take your armor off or put your sword away.

You don't get to pick when you're attacked or when you get to fight. God will rescue from every trap and protect you from deadly disease, but remember, you have to hold onto your confession even when it doesn't look like it is working. Your weapon is God's word in your mouth and planted in your heart. The attack was so severe; it made me question everything I believe. I wanted to quit and go hole up in some hole somewhere. I almost gave up. The test will come, and that is when it counts. The test gives birth to the testimony. The trial gives birth to the triumph! Great fight equals great victory! I laugh at the devil now because I have revelation from God, and it's going to be too expensive for him.

The best masters of self-defense will use their opponents' own moves and force against them. In war, when you kill the enemy, you take their weapons, their ammo, and supplies and use it against them. In Revelation 12:11 it says, "They overcame him (Satan) by the blood of the lamb and the word of their testimony!" Every test and trial that I win, *boom*, I got more ammo! More testimonies! Ha ha, devil! I am telling everyone about how it works! Woo-hoo! I am telling everyone how my God delivers me, blesses me, and is continually putting me over!

The testimony you tell will help others let them know they can be delivered as well and how to do it. You don't give up. No matter how hard it is, *you don't give up*! Remember, defeated *sucks*! This is when you have to hold fast to your confession. *You fight till you win*! And it really is just as simple as holding onto your confession. You proclaim God is going to deliver you! The more public the proclamation, the better! That's it! You don't have to know how it's going to happen, just believe and expect it. It's the fear and pride that keeps you from opening your mouth the right way! Let that go! It's God's job to fulfill his word! And let me tell you, he's good for it!

Just one of the symptoms I had was preventing me from sleeping as my arms were going numb and hurting so bad that it would wake me up. How can something be numb and hurt at the same time? I was so weak and in pain at one point. I remember not being able to take the lid off my ChapStick. Not sleeping was horrible on top of misery. The thing was, it made sense. I had taken a job at the church, and the pay and hours weren't that favorable at the time. But I had to leave my old job because my hours wouldn't work for a number of reasons, one of which was getting my youngest to school. I had gone from a job at a call center with basically no physical activity to a job where I was getting anywhere in the neighborhood of twenty to twenty-three thousands steps a day.

A couple of weeks ago, I had a day where I hit thirty thousand steps. Definitely really active. With what I was doing with all the injuries I had from the past, the job was beyond what was reasonable, and the pay wasn't worth it. Repetitive motion, working on things above my head, blah, blah, blah. By the way, God is my source, not my job. If God calls you to do something, it won't make sense, and your flesh will think of all kinds of reasons why not to do it. I had turned down this job once before because it didn't make financial sense. Anyways, my wife would ask me almost daily if I needed to do something different because she could see my pain. I was determined not to finish on failure. Then on top of everything, I had somehow injured and torn a ligament in my foot. Now I can't even walk without a walking cast on my foot.

Everyone is going to see "what a failure I am," "a great man of faith" who can't overcome this without going to the doctor, and so on. This is where a lot of people get it wrong. You do what you have to do. Remember, you don't quit; it's not a nine-inning game. You play till you *win*! Don't measure yourself to others; it will only lead to pride or jealousy, and both are a sin! You fight the good fight of faith! There is always a fight. Until Jesus comes back, there is "no there" where we don't have to engage the enemy. Faith is always going to be required, but as we develop our faith, we believe for bigger and bigger things. Bigger miracles and bigger amounts of money to attack the enemy on more fronts. Being saved is free, but spreading the "good news" to take back the property and people requires money. As long as we are here on earth, it's our job to trust God and keep moving forward and doing our part for the advancement of the kingdom of God!

So going to the doctor is expensive. God dealt with me on this. I hadn't been making the time to write and work on my book the way I should. If I don't do what he has called me to do, people will not be able to be set free, and oppression is expensive. People are in misery, and people are dying.

This book was mostly talk up to that point. So I was determined no matter what, I was not done or quitting defeated. So I looked up every scripture on strength. When you are down or at a loss, go back to the Word of God. Look in your owner's manual. Yes, the Bible! What has my creator said about it? What is my inheritance? I then get myself filled up on the word of God for that situation! I can show you in my notebook for that period of time the several pages on scriptures on strength with different translations that I would confess over my body. Included in those pages is the verse that I used for healing my foot. If you look up multiple translations for Psalms 18:36, I combined parts of two of them. I confessed, "The Lord secures my steps so my ankles don't give way."

I was relentless with confessing what I had from God. If the doctor prescribed you medicine, you wouldn't miss taking it, not if you wanted to get healed. You treat the word of God like medicine, and it will cure you of what ails you. Then I prepared what I was going to say if anyone asked me "how I was." My canned response was, "I am strong in the Lord!" My foot healed supernaturally faster than the prescribed time by the doctor. Wasn't as fast as I wanted, but I received the healing I needed. I kept saying it until I was. That's how you win!

It may not be easy sometimes, but it is simple. Every time you come against something that makes your heart sink or whatever, you get your focus back on God and his Word. Regardless of the situation, you *only* speak what God says about it. You don't focus on and say what you have! You don't call the cat when you want the dog! What you have is the physical manifestation or the culmination of every seed and weed planted in your life! Remember this, who you allow to speak into your life matters! Don't "listen" to everything that is said to you, be selective! It's time to get gardening! Be sure the soil is fertile and tilled up getting anything that shouldn't be there uprooted! Plant the right seeds with your words! And keep any words of weeds with doubt or unbelief out of there. Continually renew your mind with the word of God to fight against the thoughts that will come.

If a weed pops up, you pull it and throw it by the wayside! You only water and feed the plants you want to grow! Don't give up! Period. Don't compare yourself to anyone else either. It's so easy to feel like a failure because it seems like you are failing. You start where you are, and you just keep moving forward. In Psalms 84:7 it talks about going from strength to strength and one translation says, "They grow stronger as they go." And another says, "Stronger with every step forward." Just keep standing and moving forward. Get better and learn what works, and learn how to fight. You *are* increasing in victorious power! You are more than a conqueror; you can do all things through Christ! You *are* fruitful in every good work. You *are* strong *in* the Lord.

Until you have your harvest of what you want, you stay the course. What if it takes ten years? Where are you going to be in ten years if you don't do this? As long as we are discussing time, let's talk about one of the most important keys to faith and winning the faith fight. Your words must also be present tense and not in the future! Tomorrow never comes because when you wake up tomorrow, it's today.

Now faith is! (Hebrews 11:1) Faith must always be declared present tense!

> Now faith is the substance of things hoped for, the evidence of things not seen. (Hebrews 11:1 KJV)

Now faith is, faith is now! Faith always has to be declared present tense or past tense because it's already done in God's eyes.

You *have* your car or whatever it is you're hoping for! Faith gives substance to what you are hoping for. When I was believing to get a new car, I confessed for approximately six months, "I have a Toyota Highlander limited edition" (specific) while I was catching the bus in the freezing rain and snow. Let me tell you that's a hard confession when you are saying it while you're freezing wet and cold looking at your clock waiting for the bus to get there. I even confessed I had it at a prayer meeting one Saturday. And when someone asked about it, I felt like such a liar, but I knew that is how faith works. I answered something to the effect I don't know yet, but "it's mine."

I have that car parked out in my driveway now—when I had no car to trade in, no job time to get a loan, no money for a down payment. When my head said there is no way, I declared I had it. Faith is believing in your heart (even with doubt in your head) and saying with your mouth is how you claim what is yours! God has already provided! When I "got" my car, it was in storage. The stuff you want is in storage prepared in advance. The car belonged to my friend, Chris. It was the car I originally based my faith on. In fact, I had to not be envious at the time that he got it. One of my other close friends, Nick, just had bought a new truck as well. It would have been easy for me to be upset that everyone was getting nice new cars, and I was the one who needed one!

My car had caught on fire when someone from the auto repair shop was driving it over to test why my car was having electrical problems. That is the short story of it. Apparently you had to be anointed to drive my car, but it was no joke at the time. I had been speaking to it, keeping it on the road, but the moment someone else drove it caught on fire. And it required more money to fix than it was worth. It would have been real easy to be down and bad mouth my situation. *Faith worketh by love and you can't have unforgiveness in your heart or be in strife.* Right after Jesus is using a teaching moment in Mark that gave us you can have what you say, he tacked on this verse about unforgiveness.

And when ye stand praying, forgive, if ye
have ought against any: that your Father also
which is in heaven may forgive you your tres-

passes. But if ye do not forgive, neither will your Father which is in heaven forgive your trespasses. (Mark 11:25–26 KJV)

I wanted to be mad at the car shop and blame them. I had a car, and now I don't! They wanted to fix something that I didn't think was the main issue…blah, blah, blah. Take captive every thought not in alignment with God's word. I choose my focus, and I walk in love. And my God is greater than *any* situation. Don't focus on *wrong* things, focus on getting the *right* things. So back to "my Toyota Highlander," I knew I had to be specific, so I asked myself what would fit the needs of my family and so on. And my friend Chris's car that he had recently got seemed to fit the bill. I liked it and then asked my wife if she liked it when he showed it to us. If you are married, you want to make sure you are "in" agreement.

Again I say unto you, That if two of you shall agree on earth as touching any thing that they shall ask, it shall be done for them of my Father which is in heaven. (Matthew 18:19 KJV)

This verse works well also if you can find someone with greater faith that is in the position to believe with you. You want a believer for this not a "hoper." Hope doesn't give substance; faith gives substance.

So I printed a picture of a Toyota Highlander limited edition (specific) and put it on my fridge. Every time I walked by the fridge, I hit the picture with my hand and said, "You are mine in the name of Jesus!" I had also printed Math 18:19 and Mark 11:24.

Therefore I tell you, all things whatever you pray and ask for, believe that you have received them, and you shall have them. (Mark 11:24 WEB)

When you pray is when you have to believe you have received it. Confessing it is how you start to act as if.

When Chris first approached me about the idea of me having his car, I wasn't sure, and I still had doubt in my head like me having such a nice car. Say this with me about yourself, "I deserve nice things!" I wasn't sure about the amount of the payments either. My car had been paid off. It was going to require faith to make the payments. So Chris had received a new job that came with a new vehicle, and he was trying to pay off debt and didn't need two cars. When I called him, "walking in faith" to "claim" my car, he had just put the Highlander in storage. The funny part about this story is when Chris first bought my Highlander six to eight months prior or so, and he brought it over it to show us. He felt in his spirit that it was our car but didn't say anything at the time because it didn't' make sense.

God knew in advance that the car he bought was going to be mine. Long and glorious story shorter, I took over his payments and have the car that I desired. I have possessed the promise and have never missed a payment. In my house, every need is met with heaven's best, and it doesn't matter what my job or my wife's job is. My God supplies all my needs. The car was mine for the six months that I confessed it was mine when I was catching the bus, in the snow and freezing rain, and when everything else said otherwise. I believe if I would have said anything about it being impossible or got into envy or resentment, I would not have that car, or things wouldn't have lined up in my favor. Faith is always past or present tense. "You have it." It was already provided. God has already provided everything we need. God called the end from the beginning. It's through our knowledge of him that we "get access" to get everything we need. Yes, everything for life or everything pertaining to living a godly life—nothing missing, nothing lacking.

> According as his divine power hath given unto us all things that pertain unto life and godliness, through the knowledge of him that hath called us to glory and virtue. (2 Peter 1:3 KJV)

> Blessed be the God and Father of our Lord Jesus Christ, who hath blessed us with all spiritual

blessings in heavenly places in Christ. (Ephesians 1:3 KJV)

It's going to require you learning and or gaining the knowledge of him and being "in Christ." Remember that Christ or Jesus is the word. Your knowledge of the word is what is going to set you free and release the powers of heaven.

Also importantly, hath is past tense. God and Jesus have done all they are ever going to do for you. When my sister died, she said, "God is going to heal me." Going to, unfortunately, is always in the future. We didn't know what I know now. You can only walk in the light you have and the level of faith you have. You have to start somewhere, and there is always a level above where you are right now. You have to claim it, speak it, and act like you already have it until you do!

Now, as my pastor Rick says, don't get out in front of your skies. If you have skied, you know what that means. If you lean out too far, you are going down. Don't get ahead of your faith. Don't throw away your glasses and get in your car to drive. If you're not ready, we'll all have somewhere to go tomorrow, and it will be your funeral. Faith has to be grown. It takes more time to grow a cherry tree than to grow grass. You have to start where you are at. If you can't lift a five-pound weight, you won't lift a fifty-pound weight. Faith is the currency of the kingdom, and you can't buy a two-thousand-dollar couch with five-dollar faith. You have to crawl before you can walk and walk before you can run. Practice and grow your faith by believing and saying things you should "in the natural." Have no ability to affect change.

Start claiming good parking spaces and speaking to the weather and traffic. In 2019, I was speaking against having a bad fire season because I wanted to be able to go camping later in the summer, with my boys, and not having to deal with fires and the smoke. Among other things, I was confessing pretty much all year that it was going to be a colder wetter end of the season. Well, it snowed on my pastor Rick's birthday, September 29, 2019. Wow, seriously never thought of that, but the colder wetter end of the season is snow. Your words are important. I don't care what anyone thinks of me, I *know* my words matter!

You can't see the wind, but you can see its effects. Start looking for the effects of your words. When you start becoming successful at obtaining and receiving things by faith, look at what you said and did, and you will begin to see what works. And your faith will grow. Be bold. God, your Father, wants to bless you so much more than he is able to. God is limited by our faith. He made a way, and Jesus is the way. If you are needing healing or you are sick, know this, Jesus did all he is ever going to do for your healing. It's yours already, but you have to get it in your heart what God has "said" until it "manifests" and actually shows up in your life, like my car.

> Let us hold fast the profession of our faith without wavering; (for he is faithful that promised). (Hebrews 10:23 KJV)

Profession actually also translates into confession.

> Let us hold fast the confession of our hope without wavering; for he who promised is faithful. (Hebrews 10:23 WEB)

So it is our job or it's our profession to hold onto our confession for the one who made the promise is trustworthy.

The devil will always work to get you out of faith and out of the will of God by saying, "Has God really said?" It's our job to "attend to" or put and give God's word "first place" in our life.

> My son, attend to my words; incline thine ear unto my sayings. Let them not depart from thine eyes; keep them in the midst of thine heart. For they are life unto those that find them, and health to all their flesh. (Proverbs 4:20–22 KJV)

Jesus died and took all your (our) pain and your sickness so you don't have to "have it." Poverty, pain, and sickness are "not ours," while health, healing, and prosperity are ours!

Rejecting what is not ours and claiming what is. Taking what is good and leaving behind what is not.

> Surely he hath borne our griefs, and carried our sorrows: yet we did esteem him stricken, smitten of God, and afflicted. (Isaiah 53:4 KJV)

In the margin of my King James Bible, griefs and sorrows are translated sickness and pain. Math 8:17 (KJV) says, "That it might be fulfilled which was spoken by Esaias the prophet, saying, Himself took our infirmities, and bare our sicknesses."

Jesus took our infirmities, all the things wrong with us, and bore our sickness so we don't have to bear it. It's part of the spiritual atonement. Yes, we have so much more than forgiveness of sin. Most people and Christians believe God has forgiven our sins but don't go any further. Praise God we have forgiveness, but to stop there would leave us helpless in a world that is in dire need of help. You have the power to manifest God and his benefits. But if you don't know what those benefits are, you won't have them. Faith begins where the "will" of God is known.

We have to get in the word of God and see what is ours. Us prospering and being healed is not just for "us," it's a calling card for the world to see, come to, and know God, and "be saved"! I remember God's question, "Have I any pleasure at all that the wicked should die? saith the Lord God: and not that he should return from his ways, and live?" (Ezekiel 18:23 KJV).

God wants you to *live*! "Seek ye me, and ye shall live" (Amos 5:4). Yes, God wants you to live and live life to the fullest. Not average. Not living on "barely get along street" next to "grumble alley." You were made for so much more. And here is how to get it. Get in the Bible, and get every one of the promises God has promised us. And confess them over your life! His word is health to *all* your flesh. Yes, every part of your life! In the margin of the King James Bible in Proverbs 4:22, it says medicine. The word of God is medicine to *all* your flesh.

> Let the redeemed of the Lord say so. (Psalm 107:2)

And watch the miracles start happening. Your life will become a beautiful garden blossoming in the beauty of what God intended. "For the enemy came to 'steal, kill and destroy' but I (Jesus) have come that you might have life and life more abundant to the full and overflowing" (John 10:10). Look at how that's written. I truly believe the devil can't kill and destroy without first stealing the word of God from you. Your abundant life is waiting for you to claim it. When there is a package at the post office, you have to claim it and tell them you are here to "get it." "Show up" and "claim" what's yours. You "do" that by saying, "Yes, it's mine!" Start now with your words. Start telling the story of your life the right way, the life you want to live, and the life you were designed to live. Life no longer in defeat, but life lived in victory! You are in authority now! You are the coauthor of your life with God! You get to choose. You're a king made in the image of the King of kings and Lord of lords, and what you say matters!

You have been given the keys to the kingdom; walk in your authority, and create with God the life you've always been destined to live…now choose and speak life!

About the Author

Chuck Zaagsma is an enthusiastic motivator who has triumphed over what seemed insurmountable odds and defeat. Chuck has a great testimony of how he rose up out of the ashes of physical, financial, and emotional ruin, knocking on death's door, to a completely restored soul, free from lifelong addictions, and completely transforming every area of his life for the better.

Chuck is, first and foremost, a man of God with love and reverence for him and his Word.

Chuck is a former correctional officer and US Army and Air Force veteran. God has called him to "arm the troops" and teach his Word to his people.

Chuck is an active member of Spokane Christian Center located in Spokane, Washington, and pastored by Rick and Linda Sharkey.

Chuck is married to his beautiful wife and love of his life, Pam. Chuck has four amazing sons, Josh, Xander, Zachary, and Owen.

CPSIA information can be obtained
at www.ICGtesting.com
Printed in the USA
JSHW031308130622
26961JS00002B/97

9 781638 445340